William Penn

The Harmony of Divine and Heavenly Doctrines

Demonstrated in sundry declarations on variety of subjects preached at the

Quakers meetings in London

William Penn

The Harmony of Divine and Heavenly Doctrines
Demonstrated in sundry declarations on variety of subjects preached at the Quakers meetings in London

ISBN/EAN: 9783337411350

Printed in Europe, USA, Canada, Australia, Japan

Cover: Foto ©Lupo / pixelio.de

More available books at **www.hansebooks.com**

THE

HARMONY

OF

DIVINE AND HEAVENLY

DOCTRINES:

DEMONSTRATED

IN SUNDRY DECLARATIONS ON VARIETY
OF SUBJECTS.

PREACHED AT THE QUAKERS MEETINGS
IN LONDON.

BY WILLIAM PENN, AND OTHERS.

Taken in fhort-hand as delivered by them: and now faithfully tranfcribed and publifhed for the information of thofe who by reafon of Ignorance may have received a prejudice againft them. BY A LOVER OF THAT PEOPLE.

THE THIRD EDITION.
TO WHICH IS ADDED, HIS LIFE,
Compiled from the beft Authority.

LONDON:
Printed, and Dublin re-printed, by JOHN CHARRURIER,
No. 128, Capel-ftreet.

1795.

THE EDITOR'S PREFACE.

THE Editor of this book has spared no expence to have it neatly and correctly printed, and is thankful to the public for their encouragement. He has well founded hopes, that by re-publishing it, he will render an acceptable service to society. He has no doubt but it will prove an useful companion to all well minded persons, who ardently desire to know HIM, " in whom are hid all the treasures of wisdom and knowledge"; who wish to have their minds improved, and their hearts amended. The unaffected piety of the author; the important object of the Sermons; the excellent choice of the different subjects; the purity of the language; will all tend to make it an acquisition to literary men, especially as they were never published in IRELAND, and for obvious reasons, do not appear in WILLIAM PENN's works. To view the progress of religion in his pious mind, his conversion, and manly fortitude amidst great trials; to behold the humble follower of his

mongst

SAVIOUR leaving his native country, crossing the atlantic ocean to preach the gospel; purchasing the land at a fair price from the INDIANS, whom he considered as his brethren; framing laws in mercy and justice; founding an infant republic, which has arisen to be one of the first amongst earthly kingdoms; to reflect on the hardships and sufferings contained in these pages, of an inoffensive, peaceable body of men, who are mild and tolerant in their principles, and never persecuted any man; to see the barbarous æra of bigotry and persecution almost extinct, must deeply impress the human heart with sensations, at once awful and pleasing. The young reader will naturally draw this instructive conclusion, that " Godliness with contentment is great gain", that nothing is an affliction to a good man; that GOD is the fountain of his pleasures, the source of all his goodness; his light, his life, his strength, his ALL!

" Integrity needs no defence,
" Safe is the man who trusts to innocence".

THE
LIFE
OF
WILLIAM PENN.

WHEN the BLESSED MESSIAH first called forth the immediate followers of his person, he declared self-denial essential to discipleship, saying, "Whosoever doth not bear his cross, and come after me, cannot be my disciple," Luke xiv. 27. This path himself trod before them, setting all that should come after, an example of the most perfect patience and resignation. The faithful, in every age, have met with variety of exercises; and many of them, by their more than human constancy, neither terrified by the roughest efforts of cruelty and malice on the one hand, nor enticed by the smoothest allurements of pleasure and vanity on the other, have given convincing proofs to the world, that the GRACE, which supported them, was DIVINE.

It was this which gave WILLIAM PENN, in his early years, a solid sense of religion, and a taste of that substantial peace, which the world can neither give nor take away: this inftructed him to fee the emptinefs and vanity of earthly enjoyments, and to turn his back upon the honours, profits, and pleafures of the world, at an age moft inclinable to embrace them: this enabled him to furmount all oppofition in the fearch of TRUTH; which having found, he valued as a " pearl of " great price," and laboured in the propagation and defence of it, both by preaching and writing, almoft inceffantly for many years.

HE was born in the parifh called St. Catherine's, near the Tower of London, on the 14th day of October, 1644. His father, of the fame name, was a man of good eftate and reputation, and, in the time of the commonwealth, ferved in fome of the higheft maritime offices, as thofe of rear-admiral, vice-admiral, admiral of Ireland, vice-admiral of England, &c. in all which he acquitted himfelf with honour and fidelity. After the reftoration, he was knighted by King Charles the Second, and became a peculiar favourite of the then Duke of York: his father's care, and a promifing profpect of his fon's advancement, induced him to give him a liberal education; and the youth, of an excellent genius, made fuch early improvements in literature, that about the 15th year of his age, he was entered a ftudent at Chrift's Church College in Oxford.

Now began his ardent defire after pure and fpiritual religion to fhew itfelf (1659); of which he had before received fome tafte or relifh, through the miniftry of Thomas Loe, one of the people called Quakers; for he, with certain other ftudents of that univerfity, withdrawing from the

national

national way of worship, held private meetings for the exercise of religion, where they both preached and prayed among themselves: this gave great offence to the heads of the college, and he, being but sixteen years of age, was fined for nonconformity. Which small stroke of persecution not at all abating the fervour of his zeal, he was at length, for persevering in the like religious practices, expelled the college.

From thence he returned home (1661), but still took great delight in the company of sober and religious people; which his father knowing to be a block in the way to preferment, endeavoured both by words and blows to deter him from; but finding those methods ineffectual, he was at length so incensed, that he turned him out of doors.

Patience surmounted this difficulty, till his father's affection had subdued his anger, who then sent him to France, in company with some persons of quality, who were making a tour thither. He continued there a considerable time, till a quite different conversation had diverted his mind from the serious thoughts of religion; and upon his return, his father finding him not only a good proficient in the French tongue, but also perfectly accomplished with a polite and courtly behaviour, joyfully received him, hoping his point was gained; and indeed for sometime after his return from France, his carriage was such as justly intitled him to the character of a complete young gentleman.

Great, about this time, was his spiritual conflict (1664); his natural inclination, his lively and active disposition, his acquired accomplishments, his father's favour, the respect of his friends and acquaintance, did strongly press him to embrace the glory and pleasures of this world, then, as it were, courting and caressing him, in the bloom of youth, to accept them. Such a combined force might seem almost invincible; but the earnest supplication of his soul being to the Lord for preservation, he was pleased to grant him such a portion of his holy power and spirit, as enabled him in due time to overcome all opposition, and with an holy resolution to follow Christ whatsoever reproaches or persecutions might attend him.

About the year 1666, and the 22d of his age, his father committed to his care and management a considerable estate in Ireland, which occasioned his residence in that country. Being at Cork, he was informed by one of the people called Quakers, that Thomas Loe, whom we mentioned before, was to be shortly at a meeting in that city; he went to hear him, who began his declaration with these words, " There is a faith that overcomes the world, and there is a faith that is overcome by the world;" upon which subject he enlarged with much clearness and energy. By the living and powerful testimony of this man, which had made some impression upon his spirit ten years before, he was thoroughly and effectually convinced, and afterwards constantly attended the meetings of that people, even through the heat of persecution.

On the third of the 9th month, 1667, being again at a meeting in Cork, he, with many others, were apprehended and carried before the mayor, who observing that his dress discovered not the

Quaker

Quaker, would have set him at liberty, upon bond for his good behaviour; which he refusing, was, with about eighteen others, committed to prison. From thence he wrote to the Earl of Orrery, lord president of Munster, who soon ordered his discharge.

His imprisonment was so far from terrifying him, that it strengthened him in his resolution of a closer union with that people, whose religious innocence was the only crime they suffered for.

And now his more open joining with the Quakers, brought him under that reproachful name: his companions wonted compliments and caresses, were changed into scoffs and derision: he was a by-word, scorn, and contempt, both to professors and profane; to the latter, for being religious, and to the former for having a better than theirs.

His father being informed by a letter from a nobleman of his acquaintance, what danger his son was in of being proselyted to Quakerism, remanded him home, and he readily obeyed. Upon his return, although there was no great alteration in his dress, yet his manner of deportment, and the solid concern of mind he appeared to be under, were manifest indications of the truth of the information his father had received, who thereupon attacked him afresh: and here my pen is diffident of her abilities to describe that most pathetick and moving contest which was betwixt his father and him: his father earnestly intreating him, and almost on his knees beseeching him, to yield to his desire; he, of a loving and tender disposition, in an extreme agony of spirit, to behold his father's concern and trouble: his father threatening to disinherit

inherit him; he, humbly submitting to his father's will therein: his father turning his back on him in anger; he, lifting up his heart to God, for strength to support him in that time of trial.

And here we may not omit to give our reader a particular and observable instance of his sincerity. His father finding him too fixt to be brought to a general compliance with the customary compliments of the times, seemed inclinable to have borne with him in other respects, provided he would be uncovered in the presence of the king, the duke, and himself: this being proposed, he desired time to consider of, which his father supposing to be with an intention of consulting his friends, the Quakers, about it, he assured him that he would see the face of none of them, but retire to his chamber till he should return him an answer. Accordingly he withdrew, and having humbled himself before God, with fasting and supplication, to know his heavenly mind and will, he became so strengthened in his resolution, that returning to his father, he humbly signified, that he could not comply with his desire therein.

When all endeavours proved ineffectual to shake his constancy, and his father saw himself utterly disappointed of his hopes, he could no longer endure him in his sight, but turned him out of doors the second time. Thus exposed to the charity of his friends, having no other subsistence, (except what his mother privately sent him) he endured the cross with a christian patience and magnanimity, comforting himself with the promise of Christ, " Verily, I say unto you, there " is no man that hath left house, or parents, or
" bre-

"brethren, or wife, or children, for the kingdom of God's fake, who fhall not receive manifold more in this prefent time, and in the world to come life everlafting." Luke xviii. 29, 30.

After a confiderable time, his fteady perfeverance evincing his integrity, his father's wrath became fomewhat mollified, fo that he winked at his return to, and continuance in, his family; and though he did not publickly feem to countenance him, yet when imprifoned for being at meetings, he would privately ufe his intereft to get him releafed.

About the year 1668, being the 24th of his age, he firft came forth in the work of the miniftry, rightly called to, and qualified for, that office; being fent of God to teach others what himfelf had learned of him: commiffioned from on high, to preach to others that holy felf-denial himfelf had practifed; to recommend to all that ferenity and peace of confcience himfelf had felt; walking in the Light, to call others out of darknefs; having drank of the water of life, to direct others to the fame fountain; having tafted of the heavenly bread, to invite all men to partake of the fame banquet: being redeemed by the power of CHRIST, he was fent to call others from under the dominion of Satan, into the glorious liberty of the fons of God, that they might receive remiffion of fins, and an inheritance among them that are fanctified, through faith in Jefus Chrift.

About this time (1668), two of the hearers of one Thomas Vincent, a prefbyter in the Spittle-Yard, came over to the Quakers; their paftor

tor thereat transported with fiery zeal, (a thing fertile of ill language) railing to his auditory, accused the Quakers of holding most erroneous and damnable doctrines. This coming to W. Penn's ears, he, together with G. Whitehead, demanded of Vincent an opportunity to defend themselves and friends; a conference was agreed to be held at his own meeting-house, at which several points of doctrine were started and debated, but nothing fairly determined; from hence W. Penn took occasion to write a little book, intituled, " The " Sandy Foundation shaken," which gave great offence to some then at the helm of the church, who presently took the old method of reforming what they call error, by advancing at once their strongest argument, viz. ' An order for imprison- ' ing him in the Tower of London.'

A spirit warmed with the love of God, and devoted to his service, ever pursues its main purpose; restrained from preaching, he applied himself to writing; several treatises were the fruits of his solitude, particularly that excellent one, intituled, " No Cross, No Crown;" a book which tending to promote the general design of religion, was well accepted, and hath passed sundry impressions.

And in order to clear himself from the aspersions cast upon him, in relation to the " doctrines " of the Trinity, the incarnation and satisfac- " tion of CHRIST," he published a little book called, " Innocency with her open face," by way of apology for the aforesaid " Sandy Foun- " dation shaken." In this apology he so successfully vindicated himself, that soon after the publication

lication of it, he was difcharged from his imprifonment, which had been of about feven months continuance.

On the 15th of the 7th month this year, (1669) he fet out again from London for Ireland, took fhipping at Briftol on the 24th of the 8th month, and on the 26th arrived at Cork; where he immediately vifited his friends imprifoned there, and the next day had a meeting with them, in which they were fpiritually refrefhed and comforted together: having tarried there fome days, he went from thence to Dublin, and on the 5th of the 9th month, was at the national meeting of friends there, which was held at his lodgings. At this meeting, an account of his friends fufferings being drawn up, by way of addrefs, he prefented the fame a few days after to the lord-lieutenant.

During his ftay in Ireland, though his bufinefs in the care of his father's eftate took up a confiderable part of his time, yet was he frequently prefent at, and preached in, friends meetings, efpecially at Dublin and Cork, in one of which places he ufually refided. He alfo wrote during his refidencé there, feveral treatifes, particularly, "A Letter " to the Young Convinced." He very frequently vifited his friends in prifon, and had meetings with them; nor did he let flip any opportunity he had with thofe in authority, to folicit on their behalf: and in the begining of the 4th month, 1670, through his repeated applications to the chancellor, the lord Arran, and the lord-lieutenant, an order of the council was obtained for their releafe. Having fettled his father's concerns to fatisfaction, and done his own friends many fignal fervices, he fhortly after returned into England.

In this year 1670, came forth the conventicle-act, prohibiting diſſenters meetings, under ſevere penalties; the edge of this new weapon was preſently turned upon the Quakers, who not accuſtomed to flinch in the cauſe of religion, ſtood moſt expoſed. Being forcibly kept out of their meeting-houſe in Gracechurch-ſtreet, they met as near it in the ſtreet as they could, and William Penn there preaching, was apprehended, and by warrant from Sir Samuel Starling, then lord mayor of London, dated Auguſt 14th, 1670, committed to Newgate, and at the next ſeſſions at the Old-Bailey, was, (together with William Mead) indicted for being preſent at, and preaching to, an unlawful, ſeditious and riotous aſſembly. At his trial he made a brave defence, diſcovering at once both the free ſpirit of an Engliſhman, and the magnanimity of a Chriſtian, inſomuch that notwithſtanding the moſt partial frowns and menaces of the bench, the jury acquitted him.

Not long after this trial, and his diſcharge from Newgate, his father died, perfectly reconciled to his ſon, and left him both his paternal bleſſing, and a plentiful eſtate. His death-bed expreſſions, were very inſtructive and pathetick. He was buried in Radcliffe ſteeple-houſe in the city of Briſtol.

On 5th of the 12th month this year, 1670, being at a meeting in Wheeler-ſtreet, a ſerjeant with ſoldiers came and planted themſelves at the door, where they waited till he ſtood up and preached, and then the ſerjeant pulled him down, and led him into the ſtreet, where a conſtable and his aſſiſtants ſtanding ready to join them, they carried

carried him away to the Tower, by order from the lieutenant, then at White-Hall, to inform him of the fuccefs. After about three hours time, it being evening, he came home, and W. Penn was fent for from the guard, by an officer with a file of mufqueteers. There were feveral in company with Sir John Robinfon, the lieutenant of the Tower; namely, Sir Samuel Starling, Sir John Shelden, Lieutenant-colonel Rycraft, and others. Orders being given that no perfon fhould be admitted up unconcerned in the bufinefs, they proceeded to his examination, which continued a long time, and then Sir John Robinfon faid, " your " father Mr. Penn, was my friend, and I have a " great kindnefs for you, but I muft fend you " to Newgate for fix months."

W. P. Is that all? Thou well knoweft a larger imprifonment has not daunted me; I accept it at the hand of the Lord, and am contented to fuffer his will. Alas! you miftake your intereft; you will mifs your aim; this is not the way to compafs your ends.

J.R. You bring yourfelf into trouble; You will be the heading of parties, and drawing people after you.

W.P. Thou miftakeft, there is no fuch way as this to render men remarkable; you are angry that I am confiderable, and yet you take the very way to make me fo, by making this buftle and ftir about one peaceable perfon.

J.R. I wifh your adhering to thefe things do not convert you to fomething at laft.

W.P. I would have thee and all men to know, that I fcorn that religion which is not worth fuffer-

ring

ing for, and able to sustain those that are afflicted for it: mine is; and whatever may be my lot for my constant profession of it, I am no-ways careful, but resigned to answer the will of God, by the loss of goods, liberty, and life itself. When you have all, you can have no more, and then perhaps you will be contented, and by that you will be better informed of our innocency. Thy religion PERSECUTES, and mine FORGIVES; and I desire my GOD to forgive you all, that are concerned in my commitment, and I leave you all in perfect charity, wishing your everlasting salvation.

J. R. Send a corporal, with a file of musqueteers along with him.

W. P. No, no, send thy lacquey; I know the way to Newgate.

Being committed to this prison for six months, he filled up the time of his confinement by continual employs; and here he wrote " The Great " Case of Liberty of conscience, once more brief- " ly debated and defended," together with several other pieces of occasional controversy.

His six months imprisonment in Newgate being expired, he was set at liberty, and shortly after went over into Holland and Germany; of his ministry and services at this time in those countries, some account is given by himself in the beginning of his subsequent travels into those parts, herein-after inserted.

In the beginning of the year 1672, and the 28th of his age, he took to wife Gulielma Maria Springett, daughter of Sir William Springett, formerly of Darling in Sussex, who was killed in the time

of

of the civil wars, at the siege of Bamber; his widow was afterward married to Isaac Pennington, of Peters-Chalfont in Buckinghamshire, in whose family her said daughter was brought up; a young woman whom a virtuous disposition, joined to a comely person, rendered well accomplished.

Soon after his marriage, pitching upon a convenient habitation at Rickmersworth in Hertfordshire, he resided there with his family, often visiting the meetings of friends, and returning home again.

In the seventh month this year, he took a journey to visit his friends in Kent, Sussex, and Surrey; of which his own memorandums furnish us with an observation of that singular industry which the free ministers of the gospel exercise in the discharge of their office; for in the space of twenty-one days, he, with his companion under the like concern, were present at, and preached to as many assemblies of people at distant places, viz. Rochester, Canterbury, Dover, Deal, Folkstone, Ashford, and other places in Kent; at Lewes, Horsham, Stenning, &c. in Sussex; and at Charlewood and Rygate in Surry. Great was their service in these counties; their testimonies, effectual to the strengthening of their friends, silencing of gainsayers, and to a general edification, were received by the people with joy and openness of heart; and themselves, in the performance of their duty, filled with spiritual consolation. He gives this account of their last meeting in that journey, being at Rygate; ' The Lord sealed up
' our labours and travels, according to the desire
' of my soul and spirit, with his heavenly refresh-
' ments

'ments and sweet living power and word of life,
'unto the reaching of all, and consolating our own
'hearts abundantly.' And concludes his narrative
with these words; 'And thus hath the Lord been
'with us in all our travels for his truth, and with
'his blessings of peace are we returned, which is
'a reward beyond all worldly treasure.'

In the 12th month of this year (1675), one Matthew Hide, a person that had been very troublesome in the Quakers meetings, by opposing their ministers in their public testimony and prayers, was taken sick; and on his death-bed, being under great remorse of conscience for what he had done, he could not be easy till he had sent for some of that people, and particularly George Whitehead, to whom he expressed great sorrow for the abuses done them, declaring them to be the children of God, and begging mercy of the Lord for his wilful opposition to known truth in gainsaying them; and died penitent. This gave occasion to him to publish, as a warning to others, a narrative, entitled, "Saul smitten to the "Ground."

In the year 1676, he became one of the proprietors of West Jersey in America, and was instrumental in the first colonizing of that province by the English; for King Charles II. having given the propriety of that country to the Duke of York, he granted the same to Sir George Berkley and the Lord Carteret, the former of whom sold his part to one Edward Billing, a Quaker; whose circumstances in the world afterward declining, he transferred his right to William Penn, Gawen Lawrey, and Nicholas Lucas, in trust for the payment of

his

his debts; they accordingly allotted out and fold the lands; and many people from England tranfported themfelves, and fettling there, in a few years it became a flourifhing plantation, and fo continues. The chief town of it is Burlington, fituate on the great river Delaware. But we return to religious matters.

About this time it pleafed God to infpire the hearts of two proteftant ladies of great quality in Germany, with a fenfe of the follies and vanities of the world, and to excite them to an earneft inquiry after the knowledge of Himfelf. The one was the Princefs Elizabeth, daughter of Frederick V. Prince Palatine of the Rhine and King of Bohemia, grand-daughter to King James I. and fifter to Prince Rupert, and the late Princefs Sophia, King George the Firft's mother; the other, Anna Maria de Hornes, Countefs of Hornes, a familiar acquaintance of the faid princefs. The report of their religious inclination coming to his intelligence, who embraced every opportunity of watering the growing feeds of virtue, he fent them a letter of encouragement and confolation, exhorting thofe noble women to a conftancy and perfeverance in that holy way which the Lord had directed their feet into.

King Charles the Second, in confideration of the fervices of Sir William Penn, and fundry debts due to him from the crown at the time of his deceafe, by letters patent bearing date the 4th of March, 1680-1, granted to William Penn and his heirs that province lying on the weft fide of the river Delaware, in North America, formerly belonging to the Dutch, and called the New Netherlands;

therlands; the name was now changed by the king, in honour of William Penn, whom and his heirs he made abfolute proprietors and governors of it. Upon this, he prefently publifhes an " Account " of the province of Pennfylvania," with the kings's patent, and other papers relating thereto, defcribing the country and its produce, and propofing an eafy purchafe of lands, and good terms of fettlement, for fuch as might incline to tranfport themfelves.

He alfo drew up the fundamental conftitutions of Pennfylvania, in twenty-four articles, confented to and fubfcribed by the firft adventurers and freeholders of that province, as the ground and rule of all future government; the firft of which articles fhewing that his principal was to give, as well as take, liberty of confcience in matters of religion, we fhall tranfcribe.

THE FIRST CONSTITUTION.

'IN reverence to God, the Father of light and
' spirits, the author, as well as object, of all
' divine knowledge, faith and worfhip, I do, for me
' and mine, declare and eftablifh, for the firft funda-
' mental of the government of this country, that
' every perfon that doth or fhall refide therein,
' fhall have and enjoy the free profeffion of his or
' her faith, and exercife of worfhip towards God,
' in fuch way and manner as every fuch perfon
' fhall in confcience believe is moft acceptable to
' God; and fo long as every fuch perfon ufeth
' not this Chriftian liberty to licentioufnefs, or
'   ' the

' the destruction of others; that is to say, to speak
' loosely and prophanely or contemptuously of
' God, Christ, the holy scriptures, or religion,
' or commit any moral evil or injury against
' others in their conversation; he or she shall be
' protected in the enjoyment of the aforesaid Chris-
' tian liberty by the civil magistrate.'

In the next year, 1682, he published " The
" Frame of Government of Pennsylvania," con-
taining twenty-four articls, somewhat varying
from the aforesaid constitutions, together with certain other laws to the number of forty, agreed
on in England, by the governor and divers free-
men of the said province: of which laws one was,

' That all persons living in this province, who
' confess and acknowledge the One Almigh-
' ty and Eternal God, to be the Creator,
' Upholder and Ruler of the world, and that
' hold themselves obliged in conscience to
' live peaceably and justly in civil society,
' shall in no-wise be molested or prejudiced
' for their religious persuasion or practice in
' matters of faith and worship; nor shall they
' be compelled at any time to frequent or
' maintain any religious worship, place, or
' ministry whatsoever.'

In the sixth month, 1682, himself, accompanied with divers of his friends, took shipping for
his province of Pennsylvania, and on the 30th of
the same month, he wrote from the Downs, " A
" Farewell to England, being a Salutation to all
" faithful friends."

After

After a prosperous voyage of six weeks, they came within sight of the American coast, from whence the air, at twelve leagues distance smelt as sweet as a new-blown garden. Sailing up the river, the inhabitants, as well Dutch and Swedes, as English, met him with demonstrations of joy and satisfaction. He landed at Newcastle, a place mostly inhabited by the Dutch, and the next day he summoned the people to the court-house, where possession of the country was legally given him; he then made a speech, setting forth the purpose of his coming, and the ends of government, giving them assurances of free enjoyment of liberty of conscience in things spiritual, and of civil freedom in temporal, and recommending to them to live in sobriety and peace one with another; after which he renewed the magistrates commissions, and then departed to Upland, or Chester, where he called an assembly, to whom he made the like declaration and received their thankful acknowledgments.

In the sixth month, 1683, having been about a year in Pensylvania, he writ a letter 'To the Free 'Society of Traders of that Province, residing at 'London,' wherein he describes the country, relates the customs and manners of the Indians, the condition of the first planters, and the present state and settlement of that province, with an account of the new-laid-out city of Philadelphia.

And being no less solicitous for the spiritual good, than for the temporal advantages of his people, he writ, in the year 1684, 'An Epistle to the people 'of God called Quakers, in the Province of Penn- 'sylvania.' &c.

After

After about two years refidence there, having fettled all things in a thriving and profperous condition, he returned to England, where he arrived fafe the 12th of the 6th month, 1684.

In the year 1686 he publifhed "A farther "Account of the Province of Pennfylvania;" and about this time the duke of Buckingham having writ a book in favour of liberty of confcience, for which he was always a known advocate, a namelefs author put forth an anfwer, reflecting not only on the duke himfelf, but alfo on W. Penn, faying 'The Pennfylvanian had en-
' tered him, (i.e the duke) with his Quakeriftical
' doctrine.' W. Penn gave that anfwerer a reply, entitled, "A Defence of the Duke of Buckingham's Book of Religion and Worfhip," &c. a fmall piece; in the conclufion of which, he refers to another excellent and larger difcourfe, foon after publifhed by himfelf, entitled, "A Perfuafive to Moderation to Diffenting Chriftians, in "Prudence and Confcience, humbly fubmitted "to the King and his great Council."

On the 4th of the month called April, 1687, came forth the 'King's Declaration for Liberty of ' Confcience, fufpending the Execution of all ' Penal Laws, in Matters Ecclefiaftical;' by ' which, (though probably done in favour of the Papifts) Diffenters received a general eafe, and enjoyed their meetings peaceably. The People called Quakers, having fmarted by thofe laws more than others, could not be lefs fenfible of the prefent relief; wherefore at their next annual affembly held at London, in the third month this year, they drew up an "Addrefs of Thanks to
"the

"the King," deputing W. Penn and others to present the same.

On the fifteenth of the ninth month a meeting was appointed at Wells, and a large room at an inn, with a balcony next the street, was taken for that purpose, and the bishop duly certified of the same. The room was quickly filled, and there was also a great concourse of people in the street; so that, for the conveniency of his double auditory, W. Penn placed himself in the balcony, and thence preached to the people; but in the midst of his declaration came officers from the mayor with the following warrant, viz.

'Wells City and } To the Constables, Verderors,
'Borough.   } and Serjeants at Mace, of
                    the said City.

'WHEREAS William Penn, and several o-
 'thers called Quakers, are now riotously
'and unlawfully assembled and gathered together
'in this city, and the said William Penn is now
'preaching or teaching in an house not licensed
'according to the late act of parliament. These
'are therefore in his majesty's name to require
'you to take the said William Penn, and him im-
'mediately to bring before us to answer the pre-
'mises. Given under our hands and seals this
'15th day of November, 1695.

'Matthew Baron, Mayor.
'William Salmon.'

The officers, rudely officious, though desired to tarry till he had done, forced him away instantly
before

before the magistrates; who upon examination finding the house was certified, and that, by disturbing a lawful for an unlawful assembly, they had overshot themselves, excused the matter as well as they could, and presently dismissed him.

On the 5th of the 1st month, 1695-6, he consummated his second marriage at Bristol, with Hannah the daughter of Thomas Callowhill, and grand-daughter of Dennis Hollister, an eminent man of that city; she was a sober and religious young woman, with whom he had a comfortable cohabitation during the rest of his life, and had issue by her four sons and one daughter.

There being about this time a bill depending in the House of Lords against blasphemy, he presented to that House, "A Caution requisite in the " consideration of that bill," wherein he advises that the word BLASPHEMY be so explained, as that no ambiguous interpretation might minister occasion to malicious or envious persons to prosecute under that name whatsoever they should be pleased to call so; after which the House thought fit to drop the bill.

In the 2d month 1698, he set out, together with John Everott and Thomas Story, from Bristol, where he then dwelt, for Ireland. Some time after his arrival there, John Plympton, the tenacious Baptist disputant mentioned before, being at Dublin, published a paper, entitled, " A " Quaker no Christian," to which W. Penn replied under the title of, " The Quaker a Chris- " tian;" and the more effectually to wipe away that adversary's aspersions, he also writ and dispersed a paper entitled, " Gospel Truths held by
" the

"the People called Quakers," subscribed by himself and three others of his friends; and likewise reprinted the 8th and 9th chapters of his "Primitive Christianity revived;" which gave the people a general satisfaction that Plympton's charges were groundless.

A short time after, being at Cork, he visited the bishop, and occasionally presented him with one of the papers, called "Gospel Truths," which he then seemed to receive favourably, but afterward unexpectedly published some exceptions against it in print; to which W. Penn after his coming back to England, the same year returned an answer, being, "A Defence of a Paper, en-" titled GOSPEL TRUTHS, against the Excepti-" ons of the Bishop of Cork's Testimony."

In the sixth month this year (1698), himself with his wife and family took shipping for his province of Pennsylvania; and on the third of the seventh month following, from on board the ship lying in Cowes road, near the Isle of Wight, he took his farewell of his friends, in an epistle directed "To the People of God called Quakers, " wherever scattered or gathered, in England, " Ireland, Scotland, Holland, Germany, or in " any others parts of Europe;"

' AN EPISTLE OF FAREWELL, TO THE
' PEOPLE OF GOD CALLED QUAKERS,
' WHEREVER SCATTERED OR GATHERED,
' IN ENGLAND, IRELAND, SCOTLAND,
' HOLLAND, GERMANY, OR IN ANY
' OTHER PARTS OF EUROPE.

'MY dearly beloved, and highly esteemed
' in Christ, our heavenly head, the li-
' ving and good Shepherd of the sheep, by whom
' we have been found out (one of a family, and
' two of a tribe) and made one holy flock and fa-
' mily unto Him, in this day of his spiritual and
' glorious appearance; grace, mercy and peace,
' yea, HIS peace, which the world can neither
' give you, nor take from you, be plentifully
' multiplied amongst you from day to day; that
' an holy, harmless, and faithful people you may
' be, yielding to the Lord the fruits of his good-
' ness, by a circumspect and self-denying con-
' versation to the end.

' And now, my dear friends, whom I know
' and love, and you also whom I truly love, though
' I do not know personally, nor may be so known
' of some of you, since it has pleased the good
' and all-wise God to order my course from you,
' so that I cannot visit you, as I have often desi-
' red before I left you, this, therefore, is to be
' my brotherly farewell unto you. And surely
' my soul is bowed in humble petitions to Israel's
' God, the true, and living, and powerful God,
' that it may be WELL with you all, here and
' for ever. And, my dear brethren, this is cer-
' tain, if ye DO well, you shall certainly FARE
' well;

'well; and in the end of all your trials, trou-
'bles, and temptations, it shall be said unto you,
" WELL DONE, good and faithful servants, en-
" ter ye into the joy of the Lord." 'O it is
'that which crowns the work; not saying, but
'doing; we must not only begin, but end well;
'and hold out to the end; not be of those who
'are WEARY of well-doing, but who follow the
'Lord FULLY, as Caleb and Joshua did in old
'time, and are famed for it. So that though God
'has appeared to us, and given us many and un-
'deniable testimonies that it was HE, and not
'another, who reached our hearts, and touched
'our consciences, and brought us to confession,
'yea, and forsaking too, of that which offended
'him, in great measure, blessed be his name; yet
'we are not to stop, or take up our rest here;
'we must WATCH still, PRAY still, FIGHT still,
'that good fight of faith, till we have overcome
'the enemy of our souls; and even THEN must
'we watch and pray, and that to the end of our
'days; that we may not lose that crown of glory,
'which God, the righteous Judge, shall give to
'all those that love his appearance, and over-
'come, and persevere to the end; for, be assu-
'red, we shall reap if we FAINT not; but we
'shall faint, if WE WAIT NOT UPON GOD,
'who alone is the strength of his people.

'This, my dear friends, is that which lies with
'greatest stress upon my spirit; WATCH to your
'DAILY PRESERVATION, and be not satisfied
'unless you feel it. "Sufficient is the day for
" the evil thereof," 'said our blessed Lord.
'God

' God is not wanting: he that long stood at the
' door of our hearts, under our impenitency in
' times past, "till his locks were wet with the
" dew, and his hair with the drops of the night,"
' till we were wakened out of our carnal security,
' and came to judgment in ourselves, unto unfeign-
' ed repentance; to be sure he is not weary of wait-
' ing to be gracious now to his poor people; es-
' pecially if they are poor in spirit, and hunger-
' ing and thirsting after righteousness; and are
' not filled, overlaid and choked with the cares
' and incumbrances of this world. No, he was
' ever GOOD unto Israel, yea, unto ALL that are
' of an upright and clean HEART: wherefore,
' brethren, let your eye be to the Lord, and wait
' often upon him; walk with him, and dwell with
' him, and he will walk and dwell with you: and
' then no weapon formed against you, be it in
' particular, or in general, shall prosper; that is,
' not FINALLY. It may perhaps TRY you, and
' bruise your HEEL, as it did your Lord and Mas-
' ter's; but it shall never finally prevail against
' you, if you keep the eye of your minds to him,
' and have faith in him, who saved Daniel in the
' lion's den, and Shadrach, Meshach, and Abed-
' nego in the fiery furnace, and has upheld us to
' this day under various afflictions.

' And though Balaams there are, that may be
' hired by the Balaks of our age, to curse our Is-
' rael-family of God, of which some of us have
' been very sensible, yet this we know, THE
' SON OF GOD IS AMONG US, who commands
' the FIRE and the WATER, and the WINDS, as
' well NOW as THEN: and there is no inchant-

' ment

' ment againſt Jacob, or divination againſt Iſrael,
' that can proſper. And who knows, but even
' ſome of theſe preſent Balaams may yet live to
' ſay before they die, as others of them have done
' ſince we were a people, "How goodly are thy
'" tents, O Jacob! How pleaſant is thy dwelling-
'" place, O Iſrael!" 'But then, friends, we muſt
' KEEP our tents, we muſt be a retired and a pe-
' culiar people, and dwell ALONE. We muſt
' keep above the world, and clear of the ſpirit of
' it, and thoſe many trifles, cares, and troubles
' that abound in it, with which but too many have
' viſibly wounded and pierced their own ſouls.

' Beware of this, in the name of the Lord, and
' do not tempt GOD: it is in CHRIST ye have
' peace; in the WORLD is the trouble: keep,
' therefore, in him who has called himſelf (and
' we have FOUND him ſo) the WAY, TRUTH,
' and LIFE; and you ſhall live, becauſe HE
' lives: he the ROOT, you the BRANCHES; by
' whom you will be kept green and fruitful, bring-
' ing forth the fruits and graces of the Holy Spi-
' rit, in all your converſe and commerce, that it
' may be ſeen and ſaid, "God is with you, and
' amongſt you." O! let humility, charity, meek-
' neſs, and ſelf-denial, ſhine amongſt you; ſo will
' you come to ſit, as did the primitive Chriſtians,
' in heavenly places in Chriſt Jeſus, and be pre-
' ſerved through the noiſe, ſnares, and hurry of
' this preſent evil world.

' Much I could ſay, for my heart is open, and
' full too of divine love and matter to you; but
' time fails me: therefore, FEEL me, my dear
' friends, in that love of God which is over ſea
'and

' and land; where diftance cannot feparate, or
' time decay, nor many waters quench. In which
' love I embrace and falute you all, with the kifs
' of our heavenly fellowfhip, which the Lord
' hath given us in the bleffed TRUTH. And my
' ftrong defires are to him, that we may maintain
' our bleffed relation by the fame means by which
' we came at firft into it, viz. the true fear and
' love of God; which did not only make us care-
' ful not to offend him, but alfo to be willing to
' forfake all things that came in competition with
' him, or our duty to him.

' Oh! let this chafte fear and firft love abound
' among you, my beloved in Chrift, our bleffed
' light and life; or you will decay, wither and
' die to God, and your good beginnings; which
' God Almighty forbid.

' I know there is a ferious and diligent people
' among you, who do not only know WHEN good
' comes from the hand of the Lord, but wait up-
' on him FOR it, and that daily; that their fouls
' may be ftrengthened in the way and work of
' the Lord: and thefe can no more live without
' his prefence, his myftical and hidden MANNA,
' in their fpiritual journey to the eternal Canaan
' of God, than outward Ifrael was able to live
' without MANNA in the wildernefs, in their
' journey to their temporal Canaan. And I be-
' feech my God and my Father, and your God
' and your Father, my dear brethren, to attend
' all thefe holy waiters upon him with the good
' things of his houfe, and daily make them glad
' in his holy houfe of prayer.

' But

'But the condition of some, who pretend to follow Christ, yet are afar off, affects my spirit; for they know little of these enjoyments, and hardly eat so much as the CRUMBS which fall from CHRIST'S TABLE, and seem to satisfy themselves with a mere CONVINCEMENT OF THE TRUTH, or, at best, with a bare CONFESSION to it. Who taking up a formal going to meetings, and hearing what others have to say of the work and goodness of God in and to them, they shun the daily cross of Christ, whereby they should die daily to their earthly wills and vain affections, and overcome the world, the flesh and the devil. Oh! these are still their OWN, and not the LORD'S; and gird themselves, and go whither, and do what, they list! For which cause they are lean, barren, and unfruitful to God, and to their own souls; and worship him in the FORM only, and not in the POWER of godliness; such must needs be weak in faith, ready to slip and start aside at every windy doctrine, or sensual temptation.

'Oh! my dear friends, let me prevail with you, in this my farewell to you, to turn your minds INWARD, and wait to feel your REDEEMER, and meet him in the way of his righteous judgments; for there is no redemption but through judgment, nor conversion, but through righteousness. Come and be baptized by Christ; he will baptize you with his fire and Holy Ghost. He will scower and rinse you; for, believe me, his fan is still in his HAND, and he will, if you will LET him, thoroughly purge his FLOOR, viz. your HEARTS, and

'make

'make all things clean and new there by his Spi-
' rit and power. So will you come to find your
' intereft in Chrift, as you feel his workmanfhip
' and intereft in and over YOU: and as you thus
' come to be related to Chrift, the Heavenly
' Head, (by knowing him to be Head IN you)
' fo you will come to be related to his body, the
' church, and fee your proper memberfhip and
' fervice therein; which I pray God effect, to
' his glory, and your comfort.
' And now to the whole family and flock of
' God, in this European part of the world,
' of the fame communion, according to the
' difpenfation of God; be they young or old,
' high or low, rich or poor, wife or fimple, ftrong
' or weak, male or female, bond or free; I fend
' this parting falutation of my moft dear love in
' the TRUTH; befeeching you all to have me and
' mine in your remembrance, not only when up-
' on the mighty waters, but when in the folitary
' deferts of America, if it pleafe the Lord to bring
' us fafe thither: for I am not above the love and
' prayers of my dear brethren, knowing I need
' them, and have often found, by good experi-
' ence, that they avail much with the Lord.
' I muft LEAVE you, but I can never FORGET
' you; for my love to you has been, even as
' David's and Jonathan's, above the love of wo-
' men; and fuffer me to fay, that, to my power,
' I have from the firft endeavoured to ferve you
' (and my poor country too) and that at MY
' OWN CHARGES, with an upright mind, how-
' ever mifunderftood and treated by fome, who m
' I hear-

'I heartily forgive. Accept you my services; and ever love and remember, my dear friends and brethren,

'Your old, true, and affectionate

'Friend, Brother, and

'Servant in Christ Jesus,

'Cowes, Isle of Wight,
'weighing Anchor,
'the 3d of the 7th
'month, 1699.'

'WILLIAM PENN.

On the ninth of the same month they set sail, and were near three months out at sea; Providence, by the tediousness of their voyage, protracting the time of their arrival, until the danger of a contagious distemper, then reigning in that country, was over. Upon their coming thither, they were received with the universal joy of the inhabitants.

Being now (1700) determined to settle in his province, he applied himself to the offices of government, always preferring the good of the country and its inhabitants to his own private interest; rather remitting, than rigorously exacting his lawful revenues; so that under the influence of his paternal administration, the province was in an easy and flourishing condition; when some persons here in England, taking advantage of his absence, were endeavouring to undermine both his and other proprietary governments, under the specious pretence of advancing the prerogative of
the

the crown; and a bill for that purpofe was brought into the houfe of lords. His friends, the proprietors and adventurers here, prefently reprefented the hardfhip of their cafe to the parliament, foliciting time for his return to anfwer for himfelf; and accordingly giving him a fpeedy account how matters ftood, they preffed his coming over forthwith; with which he feeing it neceffary to comply, fummoned an affembly to meet at Philadelphia, to whom, on the 15th of September 1701, he made the following fpeech, viz.

' FRIENDS,

' YOU cannot be more concerned than I am at
' the frequency of your fervice in affembly,
' fince I am very fenfible of the trouble and charge
' it contracts upon the country: but the motives
' being confidered, and that you muft have met
' of courfe in the next month, I hope you will
' not think it an hardfhip now.

' The reafon that haftens your feffions, is the
' neceffity I am under, through the endeavours
' of the enemies of the profperity of this country,
' to go for England; where, taking advantage of
' my abfence, fome have attempted, by falfe or
' unreafonable charges, to undermine our govern-
' ment, and thereby the true value of our labours
' and property. Government having been our firft
' encouragement, I confefs I cannot think of fuch
' a voyage without great reluctancy of mind, ha-
' ving promifed myfelf the quietnefs of a wilder-
' nefs, and that I might ftay fo long at leaft with
' you, as to render every body entirely eafy and
fafe.

'safe. For my heart is among you as well as
' my body, whatever some people may please to
' think; and no unkindness or disappointment
' shall (with submission to God's providence) e-
' ver be able to alter my love to the country, and
' resolution to return and settle my family and
' posterity in it: but having reason to believe
' I can at this time best serve you and myself on
' that side of the water, neither the rudeness of the
' season, nor tender circumstances of my family,
' can over-rule my inclinations to undertake it.

' Think, therefore, (since all men are mortal)
' of some suitable expedient and provision for
' your safety, as well in your privileges as pro-
' perty, and you will find me ready to comply
' with whatsoever may render us happy by a near-
' er union of our interests.

' Review again your laws; propose new ones
' that may better your circumstances; and what
' you do, do quickly, remembering that the par-
' liament sits the end of the next month, and
' that the sooner I am there, the safer I hope we
' shall be here.

' I must recommend to your serious thoughts
' and care, the king's letter to me for the assist-
' ance of New-York with three hundred and fifty
' pounds sterling, as a frontier government; and
' therefore exposed to a much greater expence in
' proportion to other colonies; which I called the
' last assembly to take into their consideration,
' and they were pleased, for the reasons then gi-
' ven, to refer to this.

' I am also to tell you the good news of the go-
' vernor of New-York, his happy issue of his con-
ferences

'ferences with the Five Nations of Indians,
' that he hath not only made peace with
' them, for the king's subjects of that colony, but
' (as I had by some letters before desired him)
' for those of all other governments under the
' crown of England on the continent of America,
' as also the nations of Indians within those res-
' pective colonies: which certainly merits our ac-
' knowledgments.

' I have done, when I have told you, that
' unanimity and dispatch are the life of business,
' and that I desire and expect from you, for your
' own sakes, since it may so much contribute to
' the disappointment of those that too long have
' sought the ruin of our young country.'

THE ASSEMBLY'S ADDRESS.

' May it please the Proprietary and Governor,

' WE have this day in our assembly read thy
'speech, delivered yesterday in council; and
' having duly considered the same, cannot but be
' under a deep sense of sorrow for thy purpose of
' so speedily leaving us, and at the same time
' taking notice of thy paternal regard to us and
' our posterity, the freeholders of this province,
' and territories annexed, in thy loving and kind
' expressions of being ready to comply with what-
' soever expedient and provisions we shall offer
' for our safety, as well in privileges as property,
' and what else may render us happy in a nearer
' union of our interests; not doubting the per-
' formance of what thou hast been so lovingly

'pleased to promise, we do with much humility,
'and as a token of our gratitude, return unto thee
'the unfeigned thanks of this house.

'Subscribed by order of the house,

'Joseph Crowdon, speaker.'

The next month he took shipping for England, and safely arrived at Portsmouth about the middle of December; and the same month came up to London: after his return, the bill, which, through his friends solicitations, had been postponed the last sessions of parliament, was wholly dropped, and no farther progress made in that affair.

About two months after this, viz. on the eighth of the month called March 1701-2, King William died; and the princess Anne of Denmark ascended the throne, who began her reign with moderation and clemency, and declared for maintaining the act of toleration. W. Penn, being in the queen's favour, was often at court, and for his conveniency took lodgings at Kensington; where he wrote "More Fruits of Solitude, being a Se-
"cond Part of Reflections and Maxims relating
"to the Conduct of Human Life." After which he removed to Knightsbridge, over against Hyde-park corner, where he resided for some years.

In the year 1703, he wrote a preface to a book published by Dan. Philips, M. D. entitled *"Vin-
"diciæ Veritatis*, being a Defence of the Quakers
"Principles, from the Misreprentations of John
"Stillingfleet, a Clergyman in Lincolnshire:" and in the same year he published a preface to a
collec-

collection of Charles Marshall's writings, entitled, " Zion's Travellers Comforted:" and in the next year a preface to the written labours of John Whitehead; all which the reader may find in the front of the books they were designed for.

Anno 1705, he wrote a short epistle, by way of exhortation, to his friends the Quakers, being as follows, viz.

' MY DEAR FRIENDS,

' HOLD all your meetings in that which sat
' them up, the Heavenly POWER of GOD,
' both ministers and hearers; and live under it,
' and not above it, and the Lord will give you
' dominion over that which seeks to draw you
' again into captivity to the spirit of this world,
' under divers appearances: that the truth may
' shine through you, in righteousness and holiness,
' in self-denial, long-suffering, patience, and
' brotherly-kindness; so shall you approve your-
' selves the redeemed of the Lord, and his living
' witnesses in and to an evil generation. So prays
' your friend and brother through the many tri-
' bulations that lead to the rest and kingdom of
' GOD,

' W. PENN.'

In this year he again visited the meetings of his friends in the western parts of England; where he had good service, and his testimony was effectual to the information of many.

In

In the year 1706, he removed with his family to a convenient habitation, about a mile from Brentford, and eight from London, where he dwelt some years; and frequently attended the meeting at Brentford; which his friends, as well for the accommodation of his family, as the general service of their persuasion, then first appointed to be held there once a month.

In the year 1707, he was unhappily involved in a suit at law with the executors of a person who had been formerly his steward; against whose demands he thought both conscience and justice required his endeavours to defend himself. But his cause (though many thought him aggrieved) was attended with such circumstances, as that the court of chancery did not think it proper to relieve him; wherefore he was obliged to dwell in the Old Baily, within the rules of the Fleet, some part both of this and the next ensuing year, until such time as the matter in dispute was accommodated.

Now although the infirmities of old age began to visit him, and to lessen his abilities of continuing his service in the work of the ministry with his wonted alacrity; yet he travelled, as his strength and health would admit, into the west of England, as also the counties of Berks, Buckingham, Surry, and other places.

In the year 1710, the air near London not being agreeable to his declining constitution, he took a handsome seat at Rushcomb near Twyford in Buckinghamshire, where he had his residence during the remainder of his life.

In the year 1712, he was seized at distant times

with

with three several fits, suppofed to be apopleƌic;
by the laſt of which, though beyond all probability of expeƌation he furvived it, his underſtanding and memory were fo impaired, as to render him incapable of publick aƌion for the future; neverthelefs we fhall continue our annals to the clofe of his days, from the account an intimate friend hath left of his condition at the vifits he yearly made him.

In the third month 1713, the aforefaid friend being at his houfe fome days, found him to appearance pretty well in health, and chearful of difpofition, but defeƌive in memory; fo that though he could relate many paſt tranfaƌions, yet could he not readily recolleƌ the names of abfent perfons; nor could he deliver his words fo readily as heretofore; yet many fenfible and favoury expreffions came from him, rendering his company even yet acceptable, and manifefting the religious fettlement and ſtability of his mind.

At a fecond vifit made him in the fpring, 1714, he was very little altered from what he had been the laſt year. The friend accompanied him in his chariot to Reading meeting, where he fpoke feveral fenfible fentences, but was not abie to fay much. At parting he took leave of his friends with much tendernefs and affeƌion.

In the year 1715, his memory became yet more deficient; but his love to, and his fenfe of religious enjoyments, apparently continued; for he ſtill often went in his chariot to the meeting at Reading, and there fometimes uttered fhort, but found and favoury expreffions. One morning, while the friend was at his houfe, being about to go to the meeting, he expreffed his defires to the Lord,

Lord, that they might receive some good from him. This year he went to Bath, but the waters there proved of no benefit to his long-continued distemper.

In the year 1716, the said friend and another went to visit him, at whose coming he seemed glad; and though he could not then remember their names, yet, by his answers it appeared he knew their persons. He was now much weaker than last year, but still expressed himself sensibly at times, and particularly took his leave of them at their going away in these words, ' My love is ' with you: the Lord preserve you, and remem- ' ber me in the everlasting covenant!'

In the fifth month 1717, being the last visit the said friend made him, he found his understanding so much weakened, as that he scarce knew his old acquaintance, and his bodily strength so much decayed, that he could not well walk without leading; nor scarce express himself intelligibly.

After a continued and gradual declension for about six years, his body drew near to its dissolution; and on the thirtieth day of the fifth month, 1718, in the seventy-fourth year of his age, his soul, prepared for a more glorious habitation, forsook the decayed tabernacle: which was committed to the earth on the fifth of the sixth month following, at Jordans in Buckinghamshire, where his former wife, and several of his family, had been before interred.

As he had led in this life a course of patient continuance in well-doing, and, through faith in our Lord Jesus Christ, had been enabled to overcome

come the world, the flesh and the devil, the grand enemies of man's salvation; he is, we doubt not, admitted to that everlasting inheritance, which God hath prepared for his people, and made partaker of the promise of Christ, Rev. iii. 21. " To him that overcometh will I grant to sit " with me in my throne, even as I also overcame, " and am set down with my Father in his throne."

SALVATION

SALVATION FROM SIN

BY

CHRIST ALONE:

OR,

THE ARM OF THE LORD REVEALED.

A SERMON PREACHED AT THE QUAKER'S MEETING-HOUSE IN GRACE-CHURCH-STREET, LONDON, AUGUST 12. 1694.

BY WILLIAM PENN.

THE Great and Blessed God that made Heaven and Earth, the Seas and the great Fountains of the Deep, and Rivers of Water, the Almighty JEHOVAH who is from Everlasting to Everlasting, He also made *Man* and *Woman*; and his Design was to make them eternally Happy and Blessed. And therefore He made Man in his own Image; *In the Image of God created he him, Male and Female created he them:* He made them after his own Likeness Holy,

Holy, Wife, Merciful, Just, Patient, and Humble, endued them with Knowledge, Righteousness, and true Holiness. But Man and Woman through their Transgressions lost this *Image* of *God*, and with it lost their *Happiness* and *true Blessedness*, that God made them in a Capacity to enjoy.

Now in this State of MISERY into which we are *fallen*, we are come short of the *Glory of God*; and it is out of this wretched woeful State we must be brought, else we shall never see the Face of God with comfort. This is an Eternal Truth of God, and recorded in the holy Scriptures, *John* iii. 16. That *God so loved the World, that he gave his only begotten Son, that whosoever believeth in Him, should not perish, but have Everlasting Life.* God so loved the World, he gave his Son to be a *Light* unto the *World*, that all might see their Way back to God again: For Sin hath darkened the Understanding, and clouded the Mind of Man and Woman, and alienated them from the *Life of God*, and their Hearts are hardened through the Deceitfulness of Sin. But now is the acceptable Time, now is the Day of Salvation, the Day of God's Grace and favourable Visitation, wherein he visits Men and Women, illuminates their Minds and Spirits with a *Light* from Heaven, that they might see the deplorable State and Condition wherein they are, and what they are doing: It is in this *Light*, that they have a *Day of Grace* vouchsafed to them, that it may be well with them, both here and for ever. They that receive this *Light*, and come out of that which they are called from, which is *Sin*, they may come

come to enjoy *Peace* with *God*. It was *Sin* that firft feparated between *God* and *Man*; and it is *Sin* now that hinders Man from Acquaintance with the *Lord*, who brings Peace unto him: It is by this *Light*, that we are to acquaint our felves with God, that we may be at Peace. Thus faith the Lord by the Prophet, *It is Sin has feparated between me and you :* Sin hath made a *Partition Wall* between God and us, and God hath fent his Son into the World to break down this *Partition-Wall* that *Sin* hath made; that fo fallen Man might return to God, and come into *Paradife* again, out of which Sin hath caft him.

Now, none can bring us back to God, and into Favour and communion with Him, but our Lord *Jefus Chirft:* He is the *Light* and *Leader* of his People. There is no Name under Heaven by which we can be faved, but the *Name* of JESUS: It is he that faves his People from their Sins; and it is in him alone that we are bleffed: *Bleffed is he whofe Tranfgreffion is forgiven, and whofe Sin is covered:* And for the fake of Chrift alone it is, that the Lord imputeth not Iniquity to us. Now pray *Examine your felves, whether you be in the faith,* 2 Cor xiii. 5. *Prove your own felves, how that Jefus Chrift is in you, except you be Reprobates.* Examine your felves, whether you have chofen the Lord for your God, and Chrift for your Redeemer? And whether you have forfaken your Sins, and turned from your evil Ways, and anfwered the Vifitation of the Love of God in your Souls? Do you believe in the Lord Jefus Chrift, who came to feek and to fave them that were loft? He is the *Phyfician of Value,* that was wounded to

heal

heal our Wounds: He was *wounded for our Tranfgreffions, bruifed for our Iniquities, and had the Chaftifement of our Peace upon him*; *that by his Stripes we might be healed:* It is he alone that could do this. Who is fufficient for thefe Things? The Lord found out one that is fufficient; he hath *laid Help upon One that is Mighty*, that is *able to fave to the uttermoft all that come unto God by Him*. God hath given him the Spirit without meafure, and filled him with Grace and Truth, that of his Fullnefs we might all receive, and Grace for Grace: He is mighty to fave the Sons and Daughters of Men, and to give them Power to become the Children of God.

This was teftified of old, *John.* i. 12. *But as many as received him, to them gave he Power to become the Sons of God, even to them who believe on his Name.* Men want *Power* over their Sins: When *Sin* appears to be exceeding finful, they would overcome it, and be rid of it, when it is troublefome: And when they are under a deep *Conviction* of the Evil of it, and fee the woful and miferable State, that Sin hath brought Mankind into, how they have loft the Image of God, and the Favour of God; they then defire to be reftored, and brought back again into their primitive State. You that know the *Truth* of *God*, fee how the Work goes on in your Hearts, fee how the *Image* of *God* is carrying on upon you. Confider, that the Lord is a Holy God, of purer Eyes than to behold Iniquity with approbation: *There is no Peace to the Wicked*, that walk in the Broad-way, and grieve the Holy Spirit, and do not anfwer his *Divine* Call. There is a two-fold

Call

Call concerning Man, a Call to *Repentance*, and a Call to *Judgment*. The *Call* to *Repentance* is in this *Day* of *God's Visitation*; they that receive it now, that are so wise, as to answer *God's Call*, and believe in the *Son of God*, and in his inward Appearance, that obey his Voice, when they hear his Call, saying, *Come away*, come out of thy Sins, come out of the Wickedness, Filthiness, and Pollution of the World; come into the Divine Nature of the *Son* of *God*; come into his Life: Into what Life? Into the spiritual Life, the divine Life? Thou hast been dead to God and alive to the World: Now that thou may'st be dead to Sin, and alive to God, come unto him that hath all Power in Heaven and Earth committed to Him. O come unto Christ, the Dear and Blessed Son of God, in this Day of Grace and Salvation, and receive Power to overcome thy Sins! Then thou wilt be a conqueror, and overcome the Devil.

We are of our selves altogether insufficient for these Things, we are weak and impotent; and our Saviour hath told us, *Without me ye can do nothing:* We are justified freely by God's Grace, through the Redemption that is in Jesus Christ; not justified by our own Works. How great a *Contradiction* is it to charge them with the contrary, that say, They cannot *Preach nor Pray, but as the Spirit of God moveth them*. Blessed be God that hath made us sensible of our own Weakness, Emptiness, and Poverty. Our Help hath been in the *Name* of the *Lord*, who made Heaven and Earth, who hath given his Son to be an Helper, and an all sufficient Saviour to us; with him he

hath

hath given sufficient Power and Strength, whereby we are enabled to overcome the *Devil*, the Enemy of our Souls: So that we may be enabled to stand against *Principalities* and *Powers*, against spiritual Wickedness, and conquer all the Powers of Darkness, and fight the *good Fight of Faith*, and finish our Course with Joy, and keep the *Faith*: seeing there is laid up for us a *Crown* of *Righteousness*, which the Lord, the righteous Judge, shall give us at that Day; and *not only to us*, (saith the Apostle) *but unto all them that love His Appearing*. We have not an *High Priest* which cannot be touched with the feeling of our Infirmities; but was in all Points tempted like as we are, yet without Sin: Christ, our Redeemer, was tempted, that he might succour those that are tempted. When the *Devil* tempted our *Saviour* in the Wilderness, and could not prevail, he went away and left him: The *Prince* of this *World* found nothing in him, upon which he could fasten his *Temptation*. Christ will enable those that believe in him to overcome the *Devil*, and to be more than conquerors, through him that loved them: He came into the World to purge and purify his People, and to be the Author of *Eternal Salvation* to all them that believe in him, and obey him. But it is said, *He did not many mighty Works*, among some to whom he preached the Everlasting Gospel, because of their Unbelief: Many will not believe in the *inward* and *spiritual Appearance* of *Jesus Christ* the *Son of God*, who is the *Light* of the World; they will neither believe in the *Light*, nor walk in the *Light*, which will enable them to conquer the evil One, who is the

Prince

Prince of darkness: It is only through *Christ Jesus*, the great Captain of our Salvation, that we are victorious.

Therefore, my friends, open your Hearts to the Lord Jesus Christ, receive this blessed *Gift* of *God* which he offers to you: And can God give you a greater Gift, than the *Son* of his *Love?* And will not you gladly receive him, and that great Salvation which he hath purchased for you with his own *Blood!* But, say some People, we have received Christ, and believe in him, and believe the Divine Authority of the Holy Scriptures. But let me ask you, Who keeps House all this while? What have you done for Christ? Christ hath *died* for you; but hast thou *lived* to him? And hast thou died to the World, and died to thy Sins and Lusts? Consider with yourselves, It is both your great *duty* and Interest to *die* to Sin, and live to *Christ* that died for you. And we must stand at *Christ's Tribunal*, and give an Account to him, of whatsoever we have done, whether good or bad; and he will judge us at the Great Day of his Appearing. Blessed are you, that receive the blessed Son of God, that now stands in Spirit at the *Door*, and *knocks*: *Open* your Heart, and make Room for him, and let not the World keep him out; and he will come in, and sup with you, and you with him: And he will do that for you, which you cannot do for yourselves. The *spirit* is willing, but the Flesh is weak: He will give thee Power over Sin, and over the World, and over the Devil: When ever he shall assault thee with his Temptations, say, *Get thee behind me Satan, thou savourest not the Things that be of God.* When People come to be spiritually minded

minded they will *taste* and *savour* the Things, that are spiritual and heavenly: if they be not *Things of God*, do not touch with them, have nothing to do with them; but walk in the Spirit, and favour the Things of the Spirit. And hearken to the Counsel of Christ, who speaks unto you in the Name of Wisdom; *O ye simple Ones understand Wisdom, and ye Fools be of an understanding Heart; hear, for I will speak of excellent Things, and the opening of my Lips shall be right Things: Blessed is the Man that heareth me watching daily at my Gates, waiting at the Posts of my Doors: For whoso findeth me, findeth Life.* Hearken to the blessed Counsel of *Christ*, hear his Voice and obey it; They that do his Will, shall know his Doctrine: The Secret of the Lord is with them that fear him, and he will shew them his Covenant.

They that have the *saving Knowledge of God, and Christ Jesus, which is Life eternal,* they will walk in a correspondent and suitable manner to that *Knowledge,* and be holy in all manner of Conversation; They will not be only *Nominal Christians, but true Christians, Israelites* indeed, in whom there is no Guile; They will receive Christ Jesus, who is *God's Gift,* and know the Operation of his Power in their Souls. These Persons are fit to *live,* and prepared to *die*; when Christ, who is their Life, shall appear, they shall appear with him in Glory. When the Sound of the *Last Trumpet* shall be heard at the End of the World, *Time* shall be no more; *Come away!* that *Day* shall not be terrible to them that have put off the *old Man,* and put on the *new Man*; and have begun to live a new Life, and to have new Affections, new

Thoughts

Thoughts and Resolutions, and have laid up their Treasure in Heaven, where their Hearts are also: They have that *Peace*, which the World cannot give, and which Death cannot take away. Blessed are they, that take Sanctuary in the *Name* of *Jesus*, as in a strong Tower; they shall get Power over their Sins, and over the Vanity of their Minds, that *die* to *Sin*, and *live* to *God*, and feel the constraining Power and Efficacy of the Love of Christ, who hath loved them, and washed them from their Sins, in his own Blood, and made them *Kings* and *Priests* to *God*.

My Friends, Hear the *Voice of Wisdom*, who hath said; *Whoso findeth me, findeth Life, and shall obtain favour of the Lord: But he that sinneth against me, wrongeth his own Soul.* Be you early Seekers: *seek* the *Kingdom* of *God* in the first Place. The Lord calls from Heaven; *My Son, give me thine Heart:* Let thy Answer be; Lord, take my Heart, purify and cleanse it; break it, and make it New, make it fit for thy Acceptance, that I may find Favour in thy Sight. *Without me* (saith our Saviour) *ye can do nothing:* Therefore desire him to do it for thee, and to work in thee both to *will* and to *do* of his own good Pleasure. How dreadful is it to appear at the Bar of God's Justice, as *Miserable Sinners!* Those that have not *Christ*, the *Great Mediator*, to plead for them, are miserable indeed; Therefore lay hold on Christ now; believe in him, lay hold on his Power and Spirit in this *Day* of your *Visitation*. If thou art under the Power of Sin and *Satan*, thou may'st receive Power from Christ, to overcome all the Power of Darkness: If the *strong Man armed* hath got

Pos-

Poffeffion of thy Heart, Chrift will lay Siege to it; and if thou be willing to *open* the *Door*, Chrift will come in and caft out the *Strong Man*, and fpoil him of all his Goods. He will caft out the grand Enemy of thy Soul, and take Poffeffion for *Himfelf*; that thou mayeft be delivered from the *Power* of *Satan*, and from the Bondage of Corruption, and brought into the glorious Liberty of the *Sons* of *God:* And if the *Son* of *God* make thee free, thou fhalt be free indeed. For this End *Chrift* came into the World, for this Purpofe was the *Son* of *God* manifefted, that he might deftroy the *Works* of the *Devil:* And he will not lofe the Defign of his Coming, but will *finifh Tranfgreffion, and make an end of Sin, and bring in everlafting Righteoufnefs.*

Let us all come to *Chrift*, and let none deceive themfelves, and live in their Sins, and yet think to come to Heaven: *Be not deceived* (faith the Apoftle) *God it not mocked; for whatfoever a Man fows, that he fhall alfo reap: He that fows to his Flefh, fhall of the Flefh reap Corruption; but he that fows to the Spirit, fhall of the Spirit reap Everlafting Life.* Labour for a fure grounded *Hope*, a juft Hope in the Mercy of God for Pardon and Salvation; then you muft know a *Work* of *Chrift* upon you, and the Power of the Spirit of *Chrift* within you, fubduing your Will to a holy Subjection to the *Divine Will*; that you may fay with the Apoftle; *I am crucified with Chrift; neverthelefs I live, yet not I, but Chrift liveth in me; and the Life which I now live in the Flefh, I live by the Faith of the Son of God, who loved me, and gave himfelf for me.* Then the *Call* to *Judgment* will be joyful to you; for you fhall then be juftified

fied and acquitted before the whole World, at that *Great* and *General Judgment*, and have an abundant Entrance into the Everlasting Kingdom of our Lord and Saviour *Jesus Christ*, and it shall be well with you for ever. Now, *Say to the Righteous, it shall be well with him*; Not that it doth so appear at present ; for through many *Tribulations* we must expect to enter into the Kingdom of Heaven: And many are the *Troubles* of the *Righteous,* but the Lord will deliver them out of them all. So that *if in this Life only* (faith the Apostle) *we have Hope, we are of all Men most miserable*; Yet, *Say to the Righteous, It shall be well with him:* Whatsoever their Trials, Troubles and Tribulations are, the Lord will deliver them in the best Time; they have Heaven in their Eye, and they look to the Recompence of Reward. Now what hast thou in thine Eye? Is it the *High Calling* in Christ? Is this the *Mark* thou aimest at, and which thou hast in View? Is this the *Port* and *Haven*, that thou art sailing to, looking unto *Jesus*, the *Author* and *Finisher* of our *Faith* who for the Joy that was set before him, endured the *Cross*, despising the *Shame?* Heb. xii. 2. The *Apostle*, after he had been speaking of the Suffering and *Martyrdom* of those great *Saints*, of whom the World was not Worthy; Heb. xi. How that through *Faith, they subdued Kingdoms, wrought Righteousness, obtained Promises, stopt the Mouths of Lions, quenched the Violence of Fire, escaped the Edge of the Sword,* out of Weakness were made strong, waxed valiant in Fight, and turned to flight the *Armies* of the *Aliens*; of *Women*, that received their Dead to Life again, and others were *tortured*, not accepting of Deliverance, that they might obtain a *better* Resurrection

rection; Then he comes to speak of the Sufferings of our Lord *Jesus Christ*, and bids us, *Look unto him. Heb.* xii. 1, 2, 3. Wherefore *seeing we are compassed about with so Great a Cloud of Witnesses: Let us lay aside every weight, and the Sin that doth so easily beset us; and let us run with Patience the Race that is set before us, Looking unto Jesus, the Author and Finisher of our Faith: Who for the Joy that was set before him, endured the Cross, and despised the Shame, and is set down at the Right Hand of the Throne of God. For consider him that endured such Contradiction of Sinners against himself, lest ye be wearied, and faint in your Minds.* Blessed are they that can *endure* all these Things, *Shame, Reproach, Contumely* and *Disdain, Persecutions* and *Afflictions* that attend the Testimony of Jesus! Blessed are they, that can endure the *Cross*, and despise the *Shame!* It is an internal *Cross*, which thou must endure for *Christ*, or thy own Heart will reprove thee, check thee and condemn thee for it: But if thou comest to know a being *crucified* with *Christ*, thou shalt reign with him, and be raised up to eternal Glory with him. Unless thou knowest a dying to the World, and a being crucified with *Christ*, thou canst not have a well grounded Hope of Everlasting Happiness.

Therefore now, *Friends*, examine yourselves about your *Title* to *Heaven*. It is the Wisdom and Practice of the World, to examine their *Titles* and *Settlements*, and to see, they be sure, and firm, and stable before hand: So we should make sure for *Heaven* and Eternal Glory, and of an *House not made with Hands, eternal in the Heavens*, before this earthly Tabernacle be dissolved; then

for

for us to *live*, will be *Christ*, and to *die* will be Eternal Gain. Blessed are they that bear Record of the *Word* of *God*, and of the *Testimony* of *Jesus*, that bear his Name, and testify and join with him against the Spirit of the World, and the Prince of the Power of the Air. It is *within*, that thou must join with *Christ's Appearance*, that so thou mayest be *Christianized*, and thy Mind made truly *Christian*: Thou must be purified in thy Spirit, and baptized with the *Holy Ghost*, and with *Fire*, and know the powerful Operation of the Lord: They that have not Experience of the *New-Birth*, they cannot enter into the *Kingdom* of God.

O *my Friends*, set before you the *Example* of *Christ*, who was Holy, Harmless and Undefiled; his *Life* was glorious in *Holiness*: And as it becomes you, so it highly concerns you, to be *Holy* in all Manner of Conversation. For if you imitate not the *Life* of *Christ*, you cannot be saved *by his Death*: He came into the World, to Redeem you from all Iniquity, and to save you from Sin and Hell; Labour to Answer the Dignity of your *High* and *Holy Calling*, with a Conversation becoming the *Gospel* of *Christ*: For you are called to Glory and Virtue. Whatsoever *Troubles*, *Temptations* and *Tribulations*, may attend you in your Pilgrimage here below, If you be faithful and sincere, you will have *Peace* with *God* through our Lord Jesus Christ. In all your *Labours* and *Travels* on this Earth, you may look up with Joy, for you have a *Serene Heaven over* your Heads; let *Christ* be precious to you; *open* the *Door* of your Hearts to him, who is the *King* of *Glory*: He is oppressed in the *Hearts of the Unclean*, but he is exalted and lifted

lifted up in the Hearts of the Faithful: Blessed are they that set him upon his Throne in their Hearts! O learn of Christ to be meek and lowly: Your *Humility* will exalt Him, and will also exalt you at the last: *Be faithful to the Death, and you shall receive a Crown of Life:* Those that have *Eternal Life* in their Eye, and depend upon *Christ* alone for Salvation, they have laid a sure Foundation. All other Foundations will come to nothing; they are founded in *Time,* and in *Time* they will come to moulder away: But that *City* that *God* is the Builder and Maker of, that *Abraham* had in his Eye, will never decay, nor moulder away: Let us have this always in our Eye, that nothing may intercept our View. *We have here* (saith the Apostle) *no continuing City*; *We seek one that is to come.* In this World we are as *Sheep* among *Wolves: Fear not, little Flock,* (faith our Saviour) *It is your Fathers good Pleasure to give you a Kingdom.* If we be the *Sheep of Christ*, we shall follow him: For *his sheep follow him, and know his Voice, and a Stranger they will not follow, but they will flee from him, for they know not the Voice of a Stranger.* *My Sheep* (faith Christ) *hear my Voice, and I know them, and they follow Me, and I give unto them Eternal Life, and they shall never perish, neither shall any pluck them out of my Hands.* Here is Encouragement for us to labour abundantly in the *Work of the Lord*; for our *Labour* shall not be in vain in the Lord. Let us, with *Moses,* chuse rather to suffer *Affliction* with the People of God, than to enjoy the *Pleasures* of Sin for a Season; and esteem the *Reproach* of *Christ* greater Riches than

. . the

the *Treasures* of *Egypt*; and have Respect to the Recompence of Reward.

Friends, I beseech you, in the Fear of God, look up unto *Jesus*, the GREAT MEDIATOR of the new Covenant, the Author and Finisher of your Faith; that by patient Continuance in Well-doing, you may seek for Glory, Honour, Immortality, and eternal Life: Which you shall obtain, if you persevere to the End: For he that endureth unto the End, shall be saved.

Be not weary of Well-doing; for in due Time you shall reap, if ye faint not. He that hath appeared, as a *God* of *Salvation*, and a mighty Preserver of his People in all Ages of the World, and hath been so both to the Primitive *Christians*, and to all our Christian *Friends*, that are gone before us to an eternal Rest, if you faint not, but follow them, who through Faith and Patience do inherit the Promises, you shall lay down your Heads in Peace in him, when you come to die: And when Time shall be no more, you shall be for ever with the Lord.

To *God* be Praise, Honour, and Glory, who hath stretched forth his mighty Arm to save: Who is the *Arm* of the *Lord* but Christ Jesus, the Redeemer of Souls? When we had undone ourselves, and lost ourselves, in wandering and Departing from the Lord, the True and Living God, into Darkness and the shadow of Death, He stretched forth his Almighty *Arm*, to gather us, and to bring us into the *Paradise* of God again, when we were driven out by our own Sin, from the Face and Presence of the Lord. *Christ Jesus*, the Great and Good Shepherd of his Sheep, came to seek and to save them that were lost:

lost: The *lost Sheep* that have wandered from him, he will take them on his Shoulder, and bring them to his Fold: And he will make them lie down in *Green Pastures*, and lead them by the *still Waters*, and satisfy them with the *Rivers* of *Pleasure* that are at God's right Hand for evermore. He hath promised, That he will feed his Flock like a Shepherd, and gather his Lambs with his Arm, and carry them in his Bosom: I hope CHRIST JESUS, the GREAT SHEPHERD, will find some here this Day, that have gone astray, and gather them with his *Divine Arm*, and keep them by his mighty Power, through Faith unto Salvation. To Him be all *Praise, Honour, Glory, Dominion,* and *Thanksgiving:* For He alone is worthy, who is GOD over all, Blessed for Ever and Ever!

Amen.

THE
SURE FOUNDATION.

A SERMON PREACHED AT THE QUAKER'S MEETING-HOUSE IN GRACE-CHURCH-STREET, LONDON, OCTOBER 10. 1694.

BY WILLIAM PENN. WITH HIS EXCELLENT PRAYER.

THE Foundation of GOD *standeth sure*; and they that will build sure, must build upon it. This hath been God's great Love to us, in this Day, Age and Generation, that he hath laid for us this *sure Foundation*, that which in all Ages the People of God have been built upon, and have been preserved in all the *Storms* and *Tempests* that have been raised, both from *within* and *without*. They who are fellow Citizens with the Saints, and of the *Houshold* of *God*, are built upon the Foundation of the Prophets and Apostles, *Jesus Christ himself being the chief corner Stone*; in whom all the Building fitly framed together, groweth unto a Holy *Temple* in the Lord, *Ephes.* ii. 20.

   Friends, I exhort you in the Name and Power of the living God, Mind this *Foundation*, upon it do you build all your Hopes of *Salvation*. The living *Power* and *Truth* of the *Living God*, is that which visited us in the Beginning, and gathered us out of that which is Evil, into that which is *Holy*, *Pure* and *Precious:* Blessed are you that feel, and experimentally know this *Visitation* of the Lord, within you, from Day to Day, and from one Season to another: This is that wherein stands your Refreshment, your consolation, your Succour a d relief in all the Times of *Temptation* wherein t e Enemy of Souls goes about, like a *Roaring Lion, seeking whom he may devour.* This subtil Enemy is always waiting how he may break into God's Vineyard, and lay waste and spoil the *Heritage* of the *Lord*; but by his Divine Light and Spirit, and the word of his Grace, they shall be preserved. This is the *Word* which you read of in *Rom.* x. 8. and mentioned by *Moses* Deut. xxx. 14. *The Word is nigh thee, even in thy Mouth, and in thy Heart:* That is, the *Word* of *Faith* which we preach, this is that *Word* of *God* by which you and all *God's People* have been preserved in all Ages and Generations. Here is the *Foundation* of Peace and Love, of Purity and Holiness; they that come to build on this *Foundation*, they see it to be a *sure Foundation*, by the Brightness of Christ's Appearance, by the Manifestation of the Son of God. For *God, who commanded the Light to shine out of Darkness, hath shined into our Hearts, to give the Light of the Knowledge of the Glory of God, in the Face of* Jesus Christ. This is the *Foundation*; in building upon which, our Souls can find Peace and Satisfaction. This is revealed and made known by the Sovereign Almighty Arm, and Power and Wisdom of the Eternal God. This is that which I would leave among you; build upon the right *Foundation*, even upon the Lord *Jesus Christ*, the blessed *Son* of *God*. God sent his own Son in the Likeness of sinful Flesh, and for Sin condemned Sin in the Flesh; that you may all

come

come to be juftified freely, by his Grace, and led by the *Spirit* of *God*, as the Children of God : That you may walk in the *Spirit*, and not fulfil the Lufts of the *Flefh*, for *If ye live after the Flefh* (faith the Apoftle) *Ye fhall die ; but if you through the Spirit mortify the Deeds of the Body ye fhall live*, Rom. viii. 13. The *Spirit* of *God* is a Spirit of Purity, Holinefs, Righteoufnefs and Self-Denial ; that will lead you through the *Straight Gate*, and in the *Narrow Way*, that leads to life.

Friends, This is the *Work* that God hath called you to, even to build upon the Right *Foundation* ; This is the Day of God's Love, the Day of his Power, wherein you are to be a willing People that this *Work* may be carried on in your Hearts, the Knowledge you have in *Religion*, it muft be *experimental* ; for *hiftorical* Knowledge only will not do ; For that is a Knowledge of the Concern of others, and not our own. Let us highly prize and value the faving *Knowledge* of *God*, and *Jefus Chrift*, which is *Life Eternal* : Let us look unto *Chrift within* us, who is the *Light* that difcovers the Works of Darknefs, and leads us out of them. Know God's *Foundation*, and build well upon it, not *Hay* and *Stubble*, which will be confumed by *Fire*. I befeech you, in the Name of the Everlafting God, build upon the true *Foundation*, *Chrift within* you, the Hope of Glory, which is a Myftery hid from Ages and Generations. Our Lord Jefus Chrift faid to his Difciples a little before his Departure ; If I *go and prepare a Place for you, I will come again, and receive you to myfelf; that where I am, there you may be alfo*. It is he, that dwelt in the Hearts of the *Primitive Chriftians* of *Old*, and it is he, that dwells in his People now ;

He

He can open in our Hearts a living Fountain, a *Well of Water springing up unto Everlasting Life*. The Lord Jesus Christ is the great *Physician*, that can cure all our spiritual *Maladies*, and he is willing and ready to help us: Come under his Teaching, and Guidance, and he will shew you the *Path of Life*, and lead you in the Way everlasting. Behold, he stands at the Door and knocks; do you open your Hearts to him, and he will come in, and sup with you, and you with him. He is calling you to *Repentance*, to turn from Sin, and come to Him that you may have Life; He will lay Judgment to the Line, and Righteousness to the Plummet, and bring down the *Man of Sin* in us, and raise us up to the Love of God, and Faith in God; that we may deny all Ungodliness and worldly Lusts, and every thing that is contrary to the Mind of God, that so we may love the LORD our GOD with all our Heart, with all our Mind, and with all our Soul. And if we love God with all our *Minds*, we must not give our Minds to any thing else; and if we love God with all our *Might* and *Strength*, we must love nothing but in subordination to him: We must love all Things; in God, and love God above all Things, then we shall come truly to know that the *Lord* is our *God*. *Matt*. vii. 24. Our Saviour speaking of building upon the Right Foundation, *Whosoever heareth these Sayings of mine, and doth them; I will liken him to a wise Man that built his House upon a Rock,* (and this *Rock* is *Christ* himself) *and the Rains descended, and the Floods came, and the Winds blew, and beat upon that House, and it fell not; for it was founded upon a Rock.* Such an one, that heareth

eth Chrift's Sayings, and doth them, he builds upon *Chrift the Rock of our Salvation:* Upon this Foundation did the holy *Patriarchs* build; and upon this Rock and Foundation did the holy *Prophets* build.

God told *Elijah* 1 King xix. 18. *Yet have I left feven Thoufand in* Ifrael, *that have not bowed unto Baal.* Have a Care of *Idolatry*, of fpiritual Idolatry, of loving any Sin or Luft : Let *Chrift* have your Hearts, and the Strength and Flower of your Love and Affections, and build upon him alone who is the true *Foundation.* Do not content yourfelves with an external *Profeffion*; Labour to come and experience the Work of *Regeneration*, that you may know you are *born again*, born of the *Spirit*, and are paffed from *Death* to *Life*, and live in Obedience to the Commands of Chrift, for he is the Author of Eternal Salvation, to all them that obey him. Have you known the *Terrors* of the *Lord?* Afk your felves, Am I fo *terrified*, as to be perfuaded to turn from that which would turn me from God? *Am* I turned from that, which would eclipfe God's *Light* in my Soul? If thou art turned from Sin to Righteoufnefs, thou art not a *Canter*, thou art not an *Enthufiaft*; thou art a true Child of God; and a Work of *Regeneration* is not only begun in thy Soul, but thou art going on to Perfection, and thou haft laid the Foundation of *Repentance from dead Works*, and *Repentance* towards God, and *Faith* towards our Lord Jefus Chrift, our great *Mediator* and Redeemer, who is the Way, the Truth and the Life: And if thou be faithful to Death, he will give thee the *Crown* of *Life.*

Let us take heed to ourfelves, and watch againft

gainſt the Enemy of our Souls, that he may not ſeduce us and bewilder us, and make us wander and loſe our *Way*, while we are travelling through the *Wilderneſs* of this *World*, toward the heavenly *Canaan*. The ſame Almighty Arm, that brought us out of *Egypt*, will conduct us through the *Wilderneſs*, and bring us ſafe to *Canaan*: Our Heavenly *Joſhua*, the Lord Jeſus Chriſt, will be our Captain and Leader, and after all our Labours and Dangers and Conflicts with potent Enemies in our Way, he will bring us to the good Land, to that Kingdom that cannot be ſhaken; that Inheritance, that is incorruptible, and undefiled, and fadeth not away: Then we ſhall know our Lot, and ſing Praiſes, living Praiſes with Joy in our Hearts, and Harps in our Hands, and worſhip him that liveth for ever and ever, ſaying, *Bleſſing, Honour and Glory and Power be to him, that ſitteth upon the Throne, and unto the Lamb for ever and ever! Worthy is the Lamb, that was ſlain, to receive Power, and Riches, Wiſdom and Strength, Honour, Glory and Bleſſing*; Who hath redeemed us to God by his Blood, out of every Kindred, and Tongue, and People and Nation; and hath made us to our God *Kings* and *Prieſts*. We muſt now believe in the Lord Jeſus Chriſt with a *Faith* that worketh by *Love*; we cannot be ſaved by a dead Faith, but by a living Faith: And as the *Body* without the *Spirit* is dead, ſo *Faith* without *Works* is dead alſo. If we believe in the Lord Jeſus Chriſt, we ſhall be ſaved from Sin, and from the Wrath to come: *Unleſs you believe in me* (ſaid our Saviour to the *Jews*) *ye ſhall die in your Sins*. They that live in their Sins, will die in them: Bleſſed are they that mor-

tify

tify their Sins, and that die to Sin, rhat they may die in the Lord, and live for ever with the Lord! Happy are they, that are found in Chrift (in a dying Hour) not having their own Righteoufnefs they fhall be accepted of God; not for any Righteoufnefs of their own, but for the *Righteoufnefs* of *Chrift*, who hath all Righteoufnefs to juftify us, and will by his Spirit work Righteoufnefs in us, and will be Sanctification to us, *He that knew no Sin, was made Sin for us, that we might be made the Righteoufnefs of God in him*; And the Apoftle tells us, that *Chrift* is made to us of God, *Wifdom, Righteoufnefs, Sanctification* and *Redemption:* O Glory, and Honour, and eternal Renown be to our Lord *Jefus Chrift*, who is all in all to us!

O *Friends*, You that are an humble People, that mourn for Sin, that are merciful, meek and lowly, and poor in Spirit, and pure in Heart; Our Lord Jefus *Chrift* in his Sermon on the *Mount* hath pronounced a *Bleffing* on you: *Bleffed are the Poor in Spirit; for theirs is the Kingdom of Heaven: Bleffed are they that Mourn, for they fhall be comforted: Bleffed are the meek, for they fhall inherit the Earth: Bleffed are the Merciful, for they fhall obtain Mercy: Bleffed are the Pure in Heart, for they fhall fee God. Mat.* v. O *Friends*, you that have tafted, that the Lord is gracious, come unto *Chrift*, as the true and fure *Foundation*: Come unto him, as a *Living Stone*, difallowed indeed of Men, but chofen of God, and precious; you alfo as lively Stones, fhall be built up a fpiritual Houfe, an holy Priefthood, to offer up fpiritual Sacrifices acceptable to God, by Jefus *Chrift: Unto you* (faith the Apoftle) *that believe*, *Chrift is*

pre-

precious. Wherefore it is written *Isa.* 28. 16. *Thus faith the Lord God, Behold I lay in Zion for a Foundation-Stone, a tryed Stone, a precious Corner Stone, a sure Foundation.* He that believeth, shall not make haste: Trust in this sure *Foundation,* you know it hath never failed you. O lay not a new *Foundation,* depart not from this sure *Foundation,* the Lord Jesus Christ; but say unto him, as *Peter,* when many Disciples went back, and walked no more with him; *Lord, to whom shall we go? Thou hast the Words of Eternal Life.* Thus by believing in Christ, and building upon this sure *Foundation,* you will bring Honour and Glory to his blessed Name, and obtain Salvation for your immortal Souls.

Blessed is he that overcometh (not he that is overcome) *He that overcometh, shall inherit all Things.* Blessed is he that *overcometh* the *World,* that overcomes the *Devil,* and that overcometh *Sin,* that overcometh his *Lusts,* his Concupisence and all Ungodliness and Unrighteousness. *Rev.* ii. 7. *To him that overcometh, will I give to eat of the Tree of Life, which is in the midst of the Paradise of God.* It is the Desire of my Soul, that you may overcome, and be more than Conquerors, through Christ, that hath loved you, and washed you from your Sins, in his own *Blood:* And that you persevere, and continue in *well-doing* to the End of your Days, and then lay down your Heads in Peace, and enter into an everlasting Rest, where there shall be no more Death, nor Sorrow, nor Crying, nor Pain, nor Mourning; but God shall wipe away all Tears from your Eyes. And you that have been *Mourners* in *Sion,* shall sing the
Song

Song of *Moses* the *Servant of God, and the Song of the Lamb,* faying, Great and Marvellous are thy *Works,* Lord God Almighty! Juft and true are thy Ways, thou King of Saints; Who fhall not fear thee and glorify thy Name, for thou only art Holy!

Thus, *my Friends,* you will blefs the Lord for ever, that hath vifited your Souls, when you come to obtain, through our Lord Jefus Chrift, *Salvation* and *Eternal Glory*; and join with the innumerable Company of Angels, and the Spirits of juft Men made perfect, in celebrating the Praifes of his Great and Excellent Name: Who alone is Worthy; who is *God over all bleffed for evermore!* Amen.

HIS PRAYER AFTER SERMON.

MOST Blessed Glorious, Eternal and Incomprehensible Lord God, we desire to worship, and humbly adore thy Excellent Majesty, whose gracious and favourable Presence is with all THINE, that wait upon thee, and desire to serve thee in the Beauties of Holiness. Thou hast mercifully made known thyself in this DAY of thy POWER and LOVE, to a willing People, that delight to worship thee in Spirit and in Truth; the desire of whose Souls is to thee only, and to the Remembrance of thy Name, that Hunger and Thirst, and Look, and Long for thy Appearance. Blessed God, thou hast appeared, and thy Appearance is Glorious: Thou hast wonderfully appeared in the Beams of Gospel-Light and Grace, and caused not only the blessed Gospel to dawn upon us, but thou hast been pleased to make thy Glory to shine upon us in the FACE of JESUS CHRIST, the dear Son of thy Love; and by the mighty and powerful Working of thy Holy Spirit, thou hast enlightened us with the SAVING KNOWLEDGE of thee, the only true God, and Jesus Christ, whom thou hast sent, which is Life Eternal. The Desire of our Souls is after thee more, than after all Things besides thee: Lord thou hast raised these living Desires in our Souls, and fervent Breathings after thee, the living God. It is the most sincere and earnest Desire of our Souls to draw nigh to thee, that thou may'st draw nigh to us, and bless us; and that our Services may be accepted, and well-pleasing to thee through Jesus Christ. Lord, be graciously pleased to bow down thy

People

People by thy mighty Power, to a holy Submiſſion and Reſignation to thy heavenly Will; and lift up the Light of thy Countenance upon all thoſe, that breathe after Communion with thee, that are thy peculiar People, and whom thou haſt ſet apart fot thyſelf, and whom thou haſt raiſed up to be Monuments of thy Mercy, and Inſtruments of thy Praiſe. There are many here preſent can ſay, That thou haſt been very good unto them; Thou haſt cauſed Joy to ſpring up in their Souls in all the Sorrows and Troubles that have attended them. O how liberally haſt thou diſtributed of thy Light and Love! Thou haſt opened a Living Fountain, and with Living Streams thou haſt conſolated and refreſhed their Souls, under their many Trials and Temptations. O God of my Life, I beſeech thee, bleſs all thy People, all that have believed in thy dear Son, Jeſus Chriſt; Draw nigh to all thoſe that deſire to come into the Fellowſhip of thy Truth; Open thy Hand, and diſpenſe thy Mercies liberally to us, that every one of us may know, that we receive from thy infinite Fulneſs, and have all our Supplies from thee. Let us be abundantly ſatisfied with thy loving Kindneſs, which is better than Life; and fed with the hidden MANNA, and eat of that Bread that came down from Heaven, that whoſoever eats of it ſhall never die, but live for ever. Let thy mighty Arm and Power, O Lord, be revealed, and thy Love ſhed abroad upon our Hearts! Preſerve us and all thy People in the hollow of thy Hand, and under thy Pavillion, from the Fury and Rage of the Enemy, and from the Strife of Tongues. Compaſs us about with

thy

thy Favour, as with a Shield, and surround us with thine everlasting Arms, that the Enemy of our SOULS may not approach us. O Lord, frustrate the Designs of that adversary, that like a roaring Lion goes about continually seeking whom he may devour. Lord hear all those that cry to thee in the Depth of their Distresses and Afflictions, and Help and Succour, and Comfort, and Support them, and deliver them in the needful Time: Shew them the path of Life, keep them from every evil Way, and LEAD THEM IN THE WAY EVERLASTING; and let them walk therein, and not be weary and faint in their Minds; looking up to Jesus, the Author and Finisher of their Faith; who for the Joy, that was set before him, endured the Cross, and despised the Shame; who is a merciful high Priest, that cannot but be touched with the feeling of our Infirmities; that was tempted as we are, that he might succour those that are tempted. Let us follow the Captain of our Salvation, who was made perfect through Sufferings, having the Kingdom of Grace in our Hearts, and Kingdom of Glory in our Eyes; and by a patient Continuance in well doing, seek after Glory and Honour, Immortality and Eternal Life. Let thy Kingdom come in Power, and thy will be done on Earth as it is in Heaven! we pray thee, sanctify all such opportunities, as these, unto thy People, and teach them to profit, and so to hear, that their Souls may live.

We cannot open the Hearts of Men; It is Thou, O Lord alone, that canst open their Hearts: Thou hast the KEY of DAVID, that canst open, and none can shut; and shut, and none

none can open. Man can do nothing of himself;
It is thou, O Lord, that doſt all. Proſper the
Labours of thy SERVANTS in the MINISTRY
in this Nation, and in all the Nations that are
nigh, and afar off, where any are gathered to wait
upon thee: Lord, be thou in the midſt of them;
let every Plant of thine own planting grow, and
bring forth Fruit to thy Praiſe. Send forth thy
LIGHT, and thy TRUTH, and let thy glorious
Goſpel have a free Courſe, and be glorified. Be
with thoſe that cannot come to the ſolemn Aſ
ſemblies of thy People, let them be taught of
God: Thoſe that lie upon Beds of Languiſhing,
do thou heal and recover them; Let them hear
the Voice of thy Rod, and not only receive Correction, but Inſtruction, and be taught by thy
Spirit ſo to IMPROVE their Afflictions, that they
may thankfully and joyfully ſay, It is GOOD for
us, that we were AFFLICTED. Pity thoſe that
are wounded with the Senſe of their Sin, and
pour Oil into their Wounds, and ſpeak Peace
unto them, and Pardon, and waſh them in the
precious Blood of JESUS, which cleanſeth from
all Sin; and prepare them for the Everlaſting
Enjoyment of thy Self in the Region of Bleſſed-
neſs, where all Tears ſhall be wiped from their
Eyes, and Sorrow and Sighing ſhall be no more.
Let the KNOWLEDGE of the LORD cover the
Earth, as the Waters cover the Sea: Finiſh Tranſgreſſion, and make an End of Sin, and bring in
everlaſting Righteouſneſs! Lord, let the Fear
and Dread of thy bleſſed Majeſty fill the Hearts
of all the Inhabitans of this Iſland, that thou
mayeſt delight to dwell in the midſt of us, and

bleſs

bless us. O Lord God Almighty, be pleased to go along with us, to the respective Places of our Abode, and let thy Presence abide with us; and let Salvation be for Walls and Bulwarks round about us! Lord, sprinkle the Posts of the Doors of thy Servants, and sprinkle our Hearts and Consciences with the BLOOD of the IMMACULATE LAMB, that the destroying Angel may pass by: And preserve all thy People in the hollow of thy Hand, and under the wing of thy Love, that they may lie down in Peace and Safety, and extol and magnify thy Great and Excellent Name, who hast extended thy Favour to them and preserved them, when they have passed through the great Waters, and mighty Deeps, where thou hast shewed them thy wonderful Power, and great Salvation: Let their Souls magnify thy Name, and their Spirits rejoice in Thee, their God and Saviour, who didst preserve thy People ISRAEL at the Sea, even at the RED SEA, and caused the Waters on the right Hand and on the left, to stand up as a Wall, while they passed through the Sea on DRY LAND, and made their Hearts glad, and to rejoice in thy great Salvation, and Triumph in thy Praise. HONOUR and GLORY be ascribed to thy great and Holy Name, for that thou hast of late delivered thy People as in Days of Old. Let them not go back again into EGYPT; but be travelling on to the heavenly CANAAN; and in thy good Time do thou give them Rest, after all their Labours, Travels, Distresses and Troubles; and let them sit down under their Vines and Fig-Trees, and eat the Fruit of their own Labours; and of thy Bounty and Beneficence,

cence, and glorify thy Name with folemn Praifes, and a heavenly Converfation. And, blefled God, fatisfy the Defires of their Souls, with Refpect to their inward, and fpiritual State and Condition, whofe Minds are exercifed about making their CALLING and ELECTION SURE; that they may at laft obtain Life Everlafting; through Jefus Chrift our Lord. Thofe that have been gathered, and brought to the Knowledge of the Truth, let them be continued in it, and enjoy heavenly Fellowfhip and Communion with thee, and the Openings of Divine Life and Love, while they are in their Pilgrimage; that they may lay down their Heads in Peace, and render to Thee, through thy dear Son, CHRIST JESUS, thy LAMB, and our Light and Leader, (who is both our Prieft and Sacrifice) Glory, Honour, Dominion and Praife, who alone is worthy, and is God over all, blefled for ever and ever! Amen.

GOD'S CALL

TO

A CARELESS WORLD.

A SERMON PREACHED AT THE QUAKER'S MEETING-HOUSE IN GRACE-CHURCH-STREET, LONDON, OCTOBER 21. 1694.

BY WILLIAM PENN.

BLESSED are all those who have answered the call of God, and who are found in his Way, whose Way is the Way of Peace, who are not weary of well doing, but having been called of God, have obediently answered that Call, and are found diligent, as those that expect to give an Account of their deeds done in the Body, that neglect not so great Salvation, which so NUMEROUS a Part of Mankind are made Partakers of; For it is certainly true, that God hath sent his Son into the World to bless Mankind, who were all under a Curse by Nature, and Children of Wrath; God hath so loved the World, as to send his Son to bless them. But, O my FRIENDS! Who among us will come to be Blessed? Who among the Sons and Daughters of Men will come to be blessed of the blessed Son of God this Day? Who came to bless us, in turning every one of us from our Iniquities.

Friends,

Friends, I call upon you all in the Name of the Lord, come and be *Blessed*; They that receive *Jesus Christ* the eternal Son of God, receive the Blessing: O you that have received the dear and blessed Son of God, and have opened the Door of your Hearts to him and said, *O come Lord Jesus, come quickly! Thou art the chiefest of Ten Thousand, and altogether Lovely, Thou art the Desire of all Nations and most desireable to my Soul;* I have had other Lovers, but now my Soul loveth thee above all, and by thee will only make Mention of thy Name; which is that strong *Tower* that I will fly unto, and take *Sanctuary* in, at all Times: O be not *Thou far* from me when *Trouble is near*, for at what time I am afraid, I will trust in Thee, and thou wilt set me on a Rock higher than I; who art mighty to save, who art the Author of *Eternal Salvation*, that canst save me from *Sin here, and from the Wrath to come*. All you who have answered thus, the Call of God, and love the Lord Jesus Christ in Sincerity, that love His Appearing, and look and long for it, and who cannot be contented and satisfied without it, that wait for the Coming of the Lord Jesus, whom your Souls love above all, O wait for Him more than they that watch for the Morning; These are they that shall have the heavenly Dew of Divine Grace descend upon them, and they shall grow as the Lilly, and encrease with the Encreases of God, and grow strong in the Lord, and in the Power of his Might: *They that wait upon the Lord* (saith the Prophet *Isaiah*) *shall renew their strength; they shall mount up with wings as Eagles, they shall run and not be weary, they shall*

E *walk*

walk and not faint; And they shall get victory over the World, and over the Prince of the Power of the Air, and Triumph over Death and the Grave, and be able to say, O death where is thy Sting! O grave where is thy victory! And likewise say with the Apostle *Paul*, when he was ready to be offered, and the Time of his Departure was at Hand, *I have fought a good Fight, I have finished my Course, I have kept the Faith: Henceforth is laid up for me a* Crown of Righteousness, *which the Lord the Righteous Judge shall give me at that* Day; *and not to me only, but unto all them that also love his Appearing*: I have fought a Good Fight, *I have kept the Faith, and that hath kept me*; and you may further say with the same Apostle, *Forgetting the things that are behind, and reaching forth unto those Things that are before, I press forward towards the Mark of the High Calling of God in Christ Jesus.* It is the desire of my Soul that you may all be a willing People in the Day of God's Power, and be pressing forward in the Ways of God, towards the Heavenly *Canaan*. And now that you are brought out of *Sodom* and *Egypt*, you may never hanker after it again, nor go from the narrow Way that leadeth unto Life Eternal. *Remember* Lot's *Wife*; when she looked back, she became a *Pillar of Salt, a Monument of God's Displeasure.* Therefore take warning by her, you that have hastened out of *Sodom*; Look not back, linger not by the Way, but persevere to the End, that you may escape the fiery Indignation of the Almighty, which will Flame against those, and come upon them to the *uttermost*, that live and die in their Iniquities. O labour therefore

fore abundantly in the Work of the Lord, and you shall enjoy Eternal Rest after all your Labours, and you shall then find that your Labour shall not be in vain; O faint not in the Way of Holiness, that leads to Everlasting Blessedness, and you shall have the Love of God shed abroad upon your Hearts by the Holy Ghost, and Divine Refreshment from the Presence of the Lord, which will make all the Ways of God to be Ways of Pleasantness and all his Paths to be full of Peace and Joy; that Peace that *passeth Understanding*, and that Joy that is *unspeakable and full of Glory*. Therefore follow *Christ your Grand Examplar and supreme Pattern*, and be willing to *deny yourselves, and take up His Cross*, and be Crucified to the World, and let the World be crucified to you, and you will appear to be the Children of the Resurrection, who are royally descended, even of the Line and Family of *Heaven*, Children of *Light*, of the Father of *Lights*, who of his *own Will* begat you with the *Word* of *Truth*, that you should be a Kind of First Fruits of his Creatures.

Here is good News for you, and glad Tidings, that you that were Children of Wrath by Nature, may by Adoption become Heirs of the Promise, the Promise of Eternal Life, through Christ Jesus, who hath purchased Deliverance and Eternal Redemption for all that do believe in Him. Here is true Liberty and Enlargement, and an opening of the Prison Doors to all those that have a deep Sense of their Misery and Bondage. It is joyful News to a Man in a Foreign Country, that lies in Prison, and under heavy Chains, to hear the joyful Report of his Redemption, and that the

Prison shall be opened, and his Chains and Fetters taken off, and that he shall be set at liberty to return to his native Country: This is welcome Tidings, relating only to the outward Man; But here is a greater Deliverance, for it is from a worse Bondage and Captivity: Here is a Call to the World, that they will come out of the Prison and dark Dungeon wherein the Devil hath long held them in Slavery and Bondage; Christ Jesus is come from Heaven to deliver them.

O come unto Christ, who is the *Light* of the World, who will bring you out of *Darkness* into his *Marvellous Light*; and turn you from the *Power of Satan*, to the *Power of God*: Ye that were sometime *Darkness*, may be made *Light in the Lord*; you that were Children of *Wrath* and Children of the *Devil*, may become the Children of God: You that were conceived in Sin and brought forth in Iniquity you come to partake of the New Birth, and be regenerated and renewed by the Holy Ghost, and washed in the blood of Christ, which cleanseth from all Sin, that you may be made meet to enter into the Kingdom of God, into which no unclean thing shall ever enter: For alas! What is the Use of purging and washing, but to take away Stains and Spo s? O purify yourselves from all filthiness of Flesh and Spirit, perfecting Holiness in the Fear of God, and work out your own Salvation with Fear and Trembling; and come unto Christ the Author of Eternal Salvation, and trust in him, and depend upon him, by a true and lively Faith, and he will ordain Peace for you: He is the Great Peace-Maker, and will make their Peace with God that

answer

answer the Call of God. Blessed are they that come under his Sceptre, under his holy and pure Power and Government.

O Friends, Answer the Call of God, that Call that doth call thee, O Man, from thy Sin, which will certainly bring thee to Destruction, if thou doest continue in it: O hearken to this Call of God! If thou doest answer that Call, then thou wilt mind the Reproofs that are given thee by the Spirit of God, and the Light that shines in thine own Heart: Thou wilt then say, I cannot go on in that Sin that God reproveth me for doing: I cannot rebel any longer against the holy Motions of the Spirit of God. I remember such a time when I was travelling upon the Way, and another time when I was upon my Bed, my conscience reproached me, and the Lord rebuked me, and secretly reproved me for such and such a Sin as I had committed. Surely it is meet to be said unto God, *I have borne Chastisement, I will not offend any more; that which I see not, teach thou me: I have done Iniquity, and I will do no more.* Say with the Psalmist, *If thou, Lord, should'st mark Iniquity, O Lord, who shall stand! But there is Forgiveness with Thee, that thou may'st be feared.*

When you are under a sense of Sin, and feel it as an intolerable burden, you will cry out, O that he that made us would save us, and shew Mercy to us for his Son's Sake! The Mercy of God is only extended to us in the Son of his Love, Christ Jesus. Let us come unto Him that we may have Life, and have it more abundantly. Blessed are they that lay hold on the Mercy and loving Kindness of the Lord, with whom there is Mercy that he may be feared. *The Lord delighteth not in the Death of a Sinner, but that he may repent, return and Live.* When the Scribes and Pharisees brought unto Christ the Woman taken in Adultery, and said to him, *Master, this Woman was taken in Adultery, in the very Act; now Moses in the Law commanded us that such should be stoned; but what sayest thou?* Jesus said unto them, *He that is without Sin among you, let him first cast a Stone at her; and they being convicted by their own Consciences, went out one by one; When they were gone out, Jesus said unto the Woman* Where are those thine Accusers? Hath no Man condemned thee? *She said, No Man Lord. And Jesus said unto her,* Neither do I condemn thee; go and Sin no more. Here He laid the Ax to the Root of the Tree, they lived in the Profession but not in the Possession of the Truth; they went out one by one, and being accused by their own Consciences, they ceased to accuse her. Christ by his Spirit doth reprove thee for thy Sin, and bids thee go and sin no more. They only shall have the Benefit of what Christ hath done and suffered in his Outward Coming in the Flesh, that believe in him, and see the Necessity of his inward Appearance and Coming in the Spirit, and answer the same. When Christ stands and knocks at the Door of thy Heart, besure to let him in; If thou shuttest the Door of thy Heart against Christ, thou dost thereby provoke him to shut the Door of Heaven against thee. *Rom.* ii. 6. *He will render to every Man according to his Deeds*; To them who by patient Continuance in well doing seek for Glory and Honour, Immortality,

tality, Eternal Life to them; But unto them that are contentious, and do not obey the Truth, but obey Unrighteousness, Indignation, and Wrath, Tribulation and Anguish upon every Soul of Man that doth Evil; of the Jew first, and also of the Gentile: But Glory, Honour and Peace, to every Man that worketh good. There is a time to Live and a time to Die. This is the Day of God's Visitation, when God calls Men by his Spirit, and invites them to accept of Mercy. There is a time coming when he will call them to Judgment: Wo be to them that have not answered the first Call, when the second Call comes. See to it while the Spirit of the Lord strives with you. Hearken to the Voice of God, the *Oracle within*, that reproves thee and checks thee for thy Sin, and reverence the Hand of the Lord when he corrects thee, and do thou patiently bear the Indignation of the Lord, because thou hast sinned against Him. This is the Day of God's Visitation! Now he calls upon Sinners, *How long, ye simple ones, will ye love Simplicity, and the Scorners, delight in their Scorning, and Fools hate Knowledge? Turn ye at my Reproof; I will pour out my Spirit unto you, I will make known my Words unto you. Because I have called and ye refused, I have stretched out my Hand, and no Man regarded, but ye have set at nought all my Counsels, and would have none of my Reproof, I also will laugh at your Calamity, and mock when your Fear cometh; when your Fear cometh as Desolation, and your Destruction cometh as a Whirlwind, when Distress and Anguish cometh upon you; then shall they call upon Me but I will not answer, they shall seek me early but they shall*

not

not find me; but whoso hearkeneth unto me, shall dwell safely, and shall be quiet from Fear of Evil. Isa. liii. 3. *Incline your ear and come unto me* (faith the Lord) *Hear and your Soul shall live; And I will make an Everlasting Covenant with you, even the sure Mercies of* David. O live in the Fear of the Lord and you shall have Peace; Live in the Fear of God, for the Fear of the Lord is the Begining of Wisdom; It is the best Wisdom that can be; It is the Wisdom of Heaven and Eternity; It is that which promotes thy Souls Eternal Happiness. When God calls thee by the Voice of the Rod, hear the Rod, and him that hath appointed it, and say in thy Heart, O Lord I have waited for thee in the Way of thy Judgments, *I will bear thine Indignation because I have sinned against thee.* I will submit to thy Correction because I have transgressed, I have done Iniquity, I will do so no more; I have done amiss, I have been vain and foolish, but I will not return to Folly. I have forsaken the Lord, and he invites me to return, and I will return unto him.

Friends, They that will not hear God's Call in the Day of his Grace, God will not hear their Call in the Day of his Wrath; He will be so far from pitying of them, that he will mock when their Fear cometh; he will laugh at them and not regard them, and there is Reason for it: For they hated Knowledge, and did not chuse the Fear of the Lord; They would none of my Counsel, they despised all my Reproof; therefore shall they eat of the Fruit of their own Way, and be filled with their own Devices; for the turning away of the Simple shall slay them, and the Prosperity of Fools shall destroy them; This is the
Condemnation

Condemnation, that Light is come into the World, and Men love Darkness rather than Light, because their Deeds are Evil; And there is no Peace, faith my God, to the Wicked; The Sacrifices of the Wicked are an Abomination to the Lord; But unto you that fear my Name (faith the Lord) shall the *Sun* of *Righteousness* arise with healing under his Wings; And they shall be mine (faith the Lord of Hosts) in that Day that I make up my Jewels, and I will spare them as a Man spareth his own Son that serveth him. Blessed are those that in the Day of their Visitation answer the Call of God's Love, who hath sent his Son to bless us in turning every one of us from our Iniquities. There are many would be glad of the Blessing, but they say in their Hearts, This Man shall not reign over us, Christ shall not be our *King:* But let me tell thee, O Man! He will rule and govern thee, if ever he save thee; He will rule over thy Mind, and over thy Will, and Affections, and Desires; and thou must bow to his *Sceptre*, if thou wilt have any share in his *Sacrifice*. Walk in love, as Christ also hath loved us and given himself for us, an Offering and a Sacrifice to God for a sweet smelling Savour; He is called JESUS, the *Mighty Saviour*; He will both save us from Sin here and from the Wrath to come. For the Grace of God which bringeth Salvation, hath appeared to all Men, and teacheth us, that denying Ungodliness and Wordly Lusts, we should live Soberly, Righteously and Godly in this present World; You must be such, if you will obtain the Blessing; You must have a God-like Life, and be Holy in all Manner of Conversation, and you must be turned from that which turned you from God; You must be turned from Sin, or Sin will turn you into Hell. They that love Sin and will live as they list; will find that the Wages of Sin is Death, and yet when *Christ* comes to judge the World, He will only save those that have taken Him for their *Lord* as well as their *Saviour*. O those who would have Christ then, must receive Christ now, and turn to the Light of Christ in their own Consciences; *Christ is the Light of the World*, he that hath the *Light* hath *Christ*, and he that hath *Christ*, hath all that is desirable. *Behold I stand at the Door and knock*; Open the Door of thy Heart, that Christ the King of Glory may come in. O that Men would but use their Wits, and exercise their Reason and Understanding, but how contrary do they act to their own Reason? They would be saved from Death, but not from Sin, which is the Cause of it; They would not be delivered from the Cause, but only from the Effect. The Wages of Sin is Death. If thou would'st be saved from Destruction and Perdition, Thou must be saved from the Cause of it; Thou must be saved from thy Sin, which is the Root of all thy Misery. For this End Christ died and shed his precious Blood, that He might take away Sin, and if He take away Sin, He must take it away where it is, even in the Hearts of Men and Women, and there you must receive him. But if you will live in your Sins, there is no Way but you must die in your Sins; Unless Christ save from Sin here, and justify you, Sin will certainly condemn you. Be willing that Christ shall save you from

Sin

Sin now, and you will have caufe to rejoice in the great Day of Judgement, for he that is the Righteous *Judge* of the *World*, and that will fentence and condemn the wicked World, will be your *Saviour* and *Juftifier*, In that Day you that mourn now, fhall rejoice for ever, and obtain Everlafting Salvation; For Chrift is the Author of Eternal Salvation to all them that believe in him and obey him. O That will be a trying Day indeed, when the Lord Jefus fhall be revealed from Heaven with his mighty Angels in flaming Fire, taking Vengence on them that know not God, and obey not the Gofpel of our Lord Jefus Chrift, who fhall be punifhed with everlafting Deftruction from the Prefence of the Lord, and from the Glory of his Power, when he fhall come to be glorified in his Saints, and to be admired in all them that believe, faith the Apoftle Paul, 2 *Theff.* i. 7. *Becaufe our Teftimony among you was believed in that Day; Wherefore alfo we pray always for you, that God would count you worthy of his Calling, and fulfil all the good pleafure of his Goodnefs, and the Work of Faith with Power, that the Name of our Lord Jefus Chrift may be glorified in you, and you in him, according to the Grace of our God, and our Lord Jefus Chrift.* Bleffed are they which are prepared for the Coming and Glorious Appearing of our Lord Jefus Chrift; They can fay with the Apoftle, 2 *Cor.* v. 1. *For we know, that if our earthly Houfe of this Tabernacle were diffolved, we have a Building of God, an Houfe not made with Hands, Eternal in the Heavens : For in this we groan earneftly, defiring to be cloathed upon with that Houfe which is from Heaven.* It is the groan of Faith and Hope,

Hope, and of vehement Desire, to be for ever with the Lord. Those that are Regenerate and born again, they are *Looking for that blessed Hope, and the glorious Appearing of the great God and our Saviour Jesus Christ; Who gave himself for us, that he might redeem us from all Iniquity, and purify unto himself a peculiar People zealous of good Works.*

It is the Desire of my Soul, that you may all come to answer the Call of God, who hath sent his Son to bless you, and to turn every one of you from your Iniquities. Let us not turn aside to the right Hand nor to the Left but be pressing forward towards the Mark of the High Calling of God in Christ Jesus, and we shall be made Partakers of the Inheritance of the Saints in Light.

The People of *Israel* were by *Joshua's* Command all circumcised, both Old and Young, before they could enter into the Good Land, that flows with Milk and Honey; So must it be now, if you will enter the Eternal Land by our Heavenly *Joshua*, *Wherewith shall a young Man cleanse his Way?* (saith the Psalmist, *Psal.* cxix. 9.) *By taking Heed thereto according to thy Word.* Hiding the Word of the Lord in your Heart, is the circumcising of it: There must be a witnessing of the *Circumcision* in the *Heart*, before we can enter into Rest in the heavenly *Canaan*. The Word of the Lord is as a Fire, and as a Hammer, and as a circumcising Knife, the Instrument of our Purification, which takes away every Thing that is unclean, that would defile us, that we may become living Temples, prepared for the Presence of the Holy GOD.

The

The Proto-Martyr *Stephen*, when he reproved the Perfecuting *Jews* that Stoned him to Death, faid, *Ye ſtiff-necked and Uncircumciſed in Heart and Ears, ye do always reſiſt the Holy Ghoſt ; As your Fathers did, ſo do ye : Which of the Prophets, have not your Fathers Perſecuted ? And they have ſlain them which ſhewed before of the Coming of the Juſt One, of whom you have been now betrayers and Murderers.* The moſt High God dwelleth not in Temples made with Hands ; *Thus ſaith the Lord, the Heaven is my Throne, and the Earth is my Foot-ſtool. where is the Houſe that ye build unto me ? And where is the place of my Reſt ? For all thoſe Things hath mine Hand made ? But to this Man will I look, even to him that is poor, and of a contrite Spirit, and trembleth at my Word.* Therefore, my Friends, give up your Hearts to the Lord, that he may fay, *Here do I delight to dwell, This is my Habitation* ; for I have defired it ; walk in the Holy Ways of God, and his Word will be a Light to your Feet, and a Lanthorn to your Paths, and you will find the good Ways of God to be Ways of Pleaſantneſs, and all his Paths to be full of Peace. O pray with the royal Pſalmiſt, *Create in me, O God, a clean Heart, and renew a right Spirit in me* ; *Caſt me not away from thy Preſence, and take not thy Holy Spirit from me: Reſtore unto me the Joy of thy Salvation, and uphold me with thy Free Spirit* ; *Then will I teach Tranſgreſſors thy Ways, and Sinners ſhall be converted unto Thee:* People muſt be firſt converted themſelves, before they can be fit Iuſtuments to convert others. *I love them that love me*, (faith the Lord

Lord) *and they that seek me early shall find me, That seek me in the first Place, before and above all. Wash you, make ye clean, put away the Evil of your Doings from before mine Eyes: Cease to do Evil, and learn to do well; Come now, and let us Reason together* (saith the Lord) *Though your Sins be as Scarlet, they shall be white as Snow; Though they be Red like Crimson, they shall be as Wool.* This is the Call of God, hearken to it, and obey; and do not start aside like a broken Bow, for then wo unto you: *Better that a Milstone were hanged about your Necks, and you cast into the midst of the Sea,* Than be disobedient to the Lord, and live and die in your Sins, and at last be drowned in Destruction and Perdition.

O my Friends Hearken to the Call of Christ; hear and your Souls shall Live. *Doth not Wisdom cry, and Understanding put forth her Voice? Unto you, O Men I call, and my Voice is to the Sons of Men: Hear, for I will speak of Excellent Things; and the opening of my Lips shall be right Things: For my Mouth shall speak Truth, and Wickedness is an Abomination to my Lips; Receive my Instruction, and not Silver; and Knowledge rather than choice Gold; Riches and Honour are with me; Yea, durable Riches and Righteousness; I lead in the Way of Righteousness, in the midst of the Paths of Judgment; that I may cause those that love me to inherit Substance, and I will fill their Treasures.* What is this *Substance?* It is *Heavenly Treasures* in the other World, *Where neither Moth nor Rust doth corrupt, and Thieves do not break Through nor Steal.* The Immutable God, that changeth not, hath an unchangeable Inheritance for his People,

that

that cannot find Peace nor Reft in their own Hearts, till they find a Place for the God of *Jacob* to dwell in : It is their moft ardent Defire that he may dwell in their Hearts, and that they may for ever dwell with him in Heaven.

O my Friends ; Caft your Care upon the Lord, and nothing fhall be able to overwhelm you ; If you have Peace with God, he will in his Time, make your Enemies to be at Peace with you ; So that you may fit down under your own Vines, and under your own Fig Trees, and eat the Fruit of your Labours. O fay with the Pfalmift, *My Soul waiteth for the Lord, more than they that watch for the Morning, I fay, more than they that watch for the Morning, Let Ifrael hope in the Lord, for with the Lord there is Mercy, and with him there is plenteous Redemption. What I fay to you, I fay unto all, Watch,* (faith our Saviour,) *Watch and Pray that ye enter not into Temptation.* We muft watch always, and pray without ceafing; I muft not pray before I watch. Let us always be upon our Watch, and walk fo as remembring we are always in the Prefence of the *Omniprefent* God. Let us fet the Lord always before us, and confider we are under his All-feeing Eye : Let us take Heed unto our Ways, and turn our Feet unto God's Teftimonies. Let us look up to God, and fay with holy *David, As the Hart panteth after the Water Brooks, fo panteth my Soul after thee, O God. My Soul thirfteth for God, for the Living God ! When fhall I come and appear before God ? Lord thou wilt fhew me the Path of Life : In thy Prefence there is Fulnefs of Joy, and at thy Right Hand there are Pleafures for evermore.* When you are panting and breathing

after

after the inward Enjoyment of the Divine Presence, some may ignorantly call it *Enthusiasm*, say it is meerly the Effect of Melancholy; but holy *David*, the Man after God's own Heart, was such an *Enthusiast*, he did ardently pant and breathe after the Enjoyment of God's Presence: God hath made known himself in and through his well beloved Son Jesus Christ; God is in Christ, and *Christ is in us, if we are his; Examine your selves,* faith the Apostle, *Know ye not that Christ is in you except ye be, Reprobates?* If God be in Christ, and Christ Jesus be in us, to rule and govern us, we are safe and happy; he will be with us in the Time of Distress, Trouble and Tribulation; and will preserve us in the Hour of Temptation. What tho' we may meet with Storms and Tempests in our Labours and Travels on this Earth? This may encourage us, that we have a *Serene Heaven* over our Heads, and in the darkest Night of our Affliction, We may look up to the *Bright Morning Star Christ Jesus,* who is our Light and our Leader; and *if we be weary and Heavy Laden, he will give us Rest:* And if we be *wounded* with the Sense of our Sins, he is the great Physician of Souls, and the *Sun of Righteousness* that *will arise with Healing under his Wings.*

My Friends, This is the Love of God to Mankind. He will bless us in turning us from our Sin to Himself; he will turn us from Darkness to Light, and turn us from that which hath turned us from God, if we will hear Him. Let us pray and strive against Sin, and bemoan ourselves with *Ephraim,* and say, *Lord thou hast chastised me, and I was chastised, as a Bullock unaccustomed to the Yoke: Turn thou me, and I shall be turned, for*

thou

thou art the Lord my God. If we humble ourselves under the mighty Hand of God, we shall with *Ephraim* hear the Sounding of *God's Bowels,* and the Voice of God pronouncing *Peace* and *Pardon* to us: *Is Ephraim my dear Son? Is he a pleasant Child? For since I speak against him, I do earnestly remember him still, therefore my Bowels are troubled for him; I will surely have Mercy upon him, saith the Lord.* But my Friends, Notwithstanding the great Love of God to Mankind, Yet how doth the Lord complain by the Prophet, *Hear O Heavens, and give ear, O Earth, for the Lord hath spoken; I have nourished and brought up Children, and they have rebelled against me: The Ox knows his Owner, and the Ass his Master's Crib; but Israel doth not know; my People doth not consider.* The Ox and Ass, which are dull and stupid Creatures, do upbraid their Ingratitude who are not affected with the Kindness of *God,* but have forgotten him Days without Number. O Remember your Owner, Live unto him, and not to yourselves. *Ye are none of your own, Ye are bought with a Price; therefore glorify God with your Bodies, and with your Spirits, which are His.* O live unto Christ that died for you; live unto his Glory, that died for your Salvation; hereby you will come to please God, by believing in him in whom he is well pleased, and you shall have that Peace and Joy that the World cannot give nor take away. Our Saviour said to the Woman of Samaria, *If thou knewest the Gift of God, and who it is that saith unto thee, Give to Drink; thou would'st have asked of Him, and he would have given thee living Water; Whosoever shall drink of this Water, shall*
thirst

thirst again, but whosoever shall drink of the Water that I shall give him, shall never thirst, but the Water that I shall give him, shall be in him a Well of Water springing up unto Everlasting Life. They that come unto Christ, and believe in him, They shall receive living Comforts and Refreshments; he will satisfy them with living Water: These Divine sweet and refreshing Joys, are only tasted by those that believe in the Lord Jesus Christ, who will abundantly satisfy the thirsty Souls, He will give them living Waters from the Brooks of *Shilo*, the Streams whereof make glad the City of God: They that drink of these Waters, of these living Streams which they receive from Christ, the *Fountain*, shall never thirst again. *Christ is that living Fountain* that gives Refreshment and Satisfaction to all that come to Him. It is of his Fulness that we all receive, Grace for Grace. Here is a Well set open by the Living and Eternal God, a Fountain unsealed, for whoever will come, may come, and drink of the Well of the Water of Life freely.

Living Praises be given to the most blessed Everlasting God, that thus aboundeth in his Mercy towards us, and deals bountifully with us: *For God who at sundry Times and in divers Manners spake in Time past unto the Fathers by the Prophets, hath in these last Days spoken unto us by his Son; whom he hath appointed Heir of all Things, who is the Brightness of his Glory, and the express Image of his Person.* He came into the World to seek and save us that were lost, who took our Nature and Sin upon him; who hath redeemed us from the Curse of the Law, being made a

Curse

Curse for us; God hath *made him to be Sin who knew no Sin, that we might be made the Righteousness of God in Him.* He hath *suffered for us,* (saith the Apostle *Peter*) *leaving us an Example, that we should follow his Steps, who his own self bare our Sins in his own Body upon the Tree; that we being dead to Sin, should live unto Righteousness.* If we follow the Captain of our Salvation, who was made perfect through Sufferings, we shall overcome the World, the Flesh, and the Devil, and be more than Conquerers through him that hath loved us; and go out of the World triumphantly, and say with the Apostle, *I have fought a good Fight, I have finished my Course, I have kept the Faith: Henceforth is laid up for me* a Crown of Righteousness, *which the Lord the Righteous Judge shall give me at that* Day; *and not to me only, but unto all them also that love his Appearing:* To whom be Glory, Praise and Dominion, for Ever and Ever. *Amen.*

THE
PROMISE OF GOD
FOR
THE LATTER DAYS.

A SERMON PREACHED AT THE QUAKER'S MEETING-HOUSE IN WHEELERS-STREET, LONDON, OCTOBER, 21. 1694.

IN THE AFTERNOON. BY WILLIAM PENN.

MY Friends, This is the Day of God's Power and Love, the Day of Grace and Salvation; concerning which it was foretold by the Prophet, That the People of God *should have Bread in their own Houses, and Water in their own Cisterns:* All you who have answered this Day of God's Visitation, and behold the glorious Appearing of the Lord Jesus Christ in your own Hearts, that are found faithful and diligent, and trusty, with the Talents which the Lord hath intrusted you with, that you may improve them for his Glory, and your own everlasting Benefit; The Lord is this Day spreading his Table, and bringing forth his Dainties, and filling the Cup of Salvation, that he may satisfy his People as with Marrow and Fatness; and that they may celebrate

his

his Praises with joyful Lips. This is a Day wherein you may eat the Bread of Life, and drink the Water of Life; This is a Day wherein God hath promised to teach his People himself; *They shall all be taught of God, and in Righteousness and in Truth shall they be established*; that all that are *Professors of Truth* may be *Possessors* of it; Now the Way to this is to receive the Truth in the Love of it, and to love the Truth as it is in *Jesus*; yea, love it above all Things in the World. Consider, my Friends, where are your Hearts and Affections this Day? Do you love God above all? Do you love him with all your Hearts, with all your Souls, and with all your Strength? God will be served with the whole Heart, *My Son, give me thine Heart*; Examine now whether God hath your Hearts this Day; I exhort and beseech you all to give up your Hearts to God, give the *Crown* and *Diadem* to Him; let him be your *Lord*, and *Lawgiver*, and *King*, and he will save you; He will be a *Sun* and a *Shield* unto you, he will supply you with all Good, and defend you from all Evil; you shall have Refreshment from the Presence of the Lord this Day, if you appear before him in a holy and humble Frame and Disposition, which is acceptable to Him: The Lord will over-shadow you with the Wing of his Love, and he will fill the Hungry with good Things, and the Rich he will send empty away. The Lord is this Day breaking the Bread of Life, and will give it to those that come with a spiritual Appetite; and here is a *Spring* opened of *Living Waters*, for refreshing of thirsty Souls that cannot be satisfied without the

Lord

Lord Jesus Christ, and that can have no true Content, Joy or Pleasure, without the Enjoyment of God. This hath been the Stay of our Minds when we have been in great Tribulation, when the Floods of many Waters have been ready to overwhelm us. We are a People that have had abundant Experience of God's mighty Power in our Preservation and Deliverance, blessed be the Name of the Lord, whose Almighty Arm hath brought Salvation.

Friends, It is the Desire of my Soul, that you may all be Christians indeed, *Israelites* indeed, (like *Nathaniel*) in whom there is no guile; That in all your *Gatherings* you may be gathered, not to Man, not to Shadows, Ceremonies and Observations, and perishing Things, but gathered to that which is the Substance of all; I would not have you gathered to a Notion of my Experience, or others Experiences, but I would draw your Minds from all visible Things, that you may be gathered to the Lord, and his Appearance in you; and then you shall have Bread in your own *Houses*, and Water in your own *Cisterns*, according to that antient Prophecy which is fulfilled in these latter *Days*, that you may have something to rely upon, the All-sufficiency of God, who hath promised to satisfy the *Hungry* and satiate the *thirsty* Soul; *Blessed are they which hunger and thirst after Righteousness, for they shall be filled:* It is the full *Soul* that *loaths* the Honey-Comb. Those that are over-charged with the World, and the Things of the World, they are of an ill Constitution; they are so filled with the World, that they cannot hunger and thirst after

Righ-

Righteoufnefs. The *Lord* fills the *Hungry* with good Things, but they that are *Rich* and *Full*, and think they *want nothing*, he fends empty away.

Martha was too intent upon the World, fhe was too folicitous and over careful, and cumbred about many Things.; fhe was very bufy in making Provifion for entertaining the Lord Jefus Chrift, and was troubled that *Mary* her Sifter did not come and help her, and complains of her to our Saviour, who was pleafed with *Mary*'s Heavenly-mindednefs, for fhe fat at Jefus's Feet, and heard him preach the Everlafting Gofpel, wanting His Bread more than he wanted hers. *Luke* x. 40. *When* Martha *was cumbred about much ferving, and faid to Chrift, Lord, doft thou not care that my Sifter hath left me to ferve alone? Bid her therefore that fhe help me: and Jefus anfwered and faid unto her,* Martha, Martha, *Thou art careful and troubled about many Things; but one Thing is needful, and* Mary *hath chofen that good Part, which fhall not be taken away from her.* Martha was concerned chiefly for the outward Entertainment of Chrift, which in itfelf was well, and a Teftimony of Love to the defpifed *Meffiah*; but fhe looked too much outward, and was over careful, and too little regarded his inward Fulnefs.; But *Mary* looked inward, to be filled and fatisfied from him, to receive of his Fulnefs, *Even Grace for Grace*, from the Living Fountain of it. *Friends*, I would have you, with *Mary*, to chufe the better Part, that you may be filled with Divine Confolations. This is that which the Lord hath opened to you this Day; Receive this bleffed

sed Treasure that will enrich you, and fill and satisfy you, and empty you of all that is contrary to itself, *viz.* The inordinate Love of earthly and perishing Things; This will beautify and adorn you with that which will render you amiable in the Sight of God; For *the King's Daughter is all glorious within:* I wonder that there are so many that are all for trimming and adorning the out-side, when *(the King's Daughter)* all those that are called of God, and sanctified by his Spirit, *are Glorious within*; these will open the Door of their Hearts to Christ, who is the *King of Glory.* Now that they may be espoused and married to Christ, they must have this heavenly Adorning from the blessed Spirit of *God,* who will beautify them with *Faith* and *Love, Holiness, Patience, Meekness, Humility,* and all other *Heavenly Graces,* which will make them *all Glorious within.* Open the Door of your Hearts to Christ the King of Glory, who hath long waited and called upon you to open to him, till his Head hath been filled with Dew, and his Locks with the Drops of the Night. If you open the Door of your Hearts to him, he will come in and sup with you, and you with him; he will beautify and adorn you, and impress his Divine Image upon you, and take away every Spot and Wrinkle, that you may appear amiable to him. Those that are true Disciples of Christ, will take up his Cross and follow him, and learn of him to be meek and lowly, then they shall find Rest to their Souls, and know by Experience that his *Yoke is easy, and His Burden light.* Receive the Truth therefore in the Love of it, and

walk

walk in it, and you will be kept out of all that is Evil, and the Blessing of the God of Heaven will rest upon you, and *the Lord will give Grace and Glory, and no good Thing will he with-hold from them that walk uprightly.* Therefore wait upon the Lord with Singleness and Uprightness of Heart, and desire in all your Meetings to meet with God, and you shall feed upon the Bread of Life, and drink of the Cup of Blessing, and the Lord will minister and dispense to every one of you according to your Necessities.

The Lord propounds and offers to our Minds nothing below Himself, we must choose Him alone for our Portion, and we shall receive from His Hands, that which is satisfying. *One Thing* (saith the Psalmist, *Psal.* xxvii. 4.) *have I desired of the Lord, that will I seek after, That I may dwell in the House of the Lord all the Days of my Life, to behold the Beauty of the Lord, and enquire in His Temple: For in the Time of Trouble he shall hide me in his Pavilion, in the Secret of his Tabernacle he shall hide me, and he shall set me upon a Rock:* Where is there a better Dwelling to abide in, and take up your Rest, than where *God* would have you dwell? *God* himself will be your *Dwelling Place in all Generations,* and be All in All to you.

Come away, O you weary and heavy laden, to Christ, and he will give Rest to your *Souls;* Make that blessed Choice that *Mary* did; chuse that *Good Part which shall not be taken from you;* You shall encrease with the Encreases of *God,* and grow up as Calves of the Stall. Let your living Cries ascend to the Living God, who heareth the

Cry of the Humble, and of those that are sensible of their low Estate; and with Strong Cries and Supplications desire to be made more alive unto God; Let the Desire of your Souls be to him, and to the remembrance of his Name. Let no *Delilah*, no darling Sin, lodge in your Bosoms to draw a-way your Hearts, and the Prime and Flower of your Affections from Christ, who is the most worthy and Supreme Object of your Love, and *altogether Lovely*, and *the Chiefest of Ten Thousands*; Let nothing obstruct the vigorous Motion of your Souls after Him. When he draws you with the Cords of his Love, do you run after Him; and let your Affections be set on Him, and fixed on Him, and He will fill you with *Joy unspeakable and full of Glory*.

My Friends, see that ye be a willing People, and a Living People; God is not straitened towards us, let not us be straitened in our own Bowels, and we shall feel His Almighty Arm supporting of us, and His bountiful Hand Communicating and reaching out good Things to us; we shall have Refreshment from the Presence of the Lord, and know that He is in the midst of us; He will *Justify us freely by his Grace, through the Redemption that is in Jesus Christ; Whom God hath set forth to be a Propitiation through Faith in his Blood, to declare his Righteousness for the Remission of Sins that are past, through the Forbearance of God; to declare, I say, at this Time His Righteousness, that He might be just, and the Justifier of him which believeth in Jesus.*

My

My Friends, If we set our Affections on Things above, and seek first the Kingdom of God, and the Righteousness thereof, all other Things shall be added to us; for *Godliness is profitable to all Things, having the Promise of the Life that now is, and of that which is to come.* Blessed are they that can witness and experience a Work of God upon their Souls, changing them and renewing them, in the Spirit of their Minds, and conforming them to the Divine Image and Will, and putting his Fear into their Hearts, that they may never depart from Him. The Angel of the Lord encampeth round about them that fear Him, and delivers them; *O taste and see that the Lord is Good! Blessed is the Man that trusteth in Him! The Eyes of the Lord are upon the Righteous, and his Ear is open to their Cry*; He will give them whatsoever they want, and deny them nothing that is good for them. If they want Faith, Patience, Courage, Humilty, Self-denial, or any other Grace of the Spirit, he will give it to them; If they want Victory over Temptation, and Strength to subdue Corruption, or to bear Tribulation, or Persecution, or Reproach, for the Name of Christ, the Lord will answer the Desire of their Souls. O the Besetments, and Snares, and Stratagems of the Devil, the grand Enemy of our Souls! We are attacked and assaulted on all Hands, let us not be discouraged, but travel on in the undefiled Way, that will bring us to an undefiled and Eternal Rest. Let us forsake Sin, and the Vanities of the World, and go up to the House of the Lord, the place where His Honour dwells; Let us encourage one another, and pro-

F 2 voke

voke one another to Love and good Works, and walk in the Way of Holiness, having our Loins girt; Let us so run, that we may obtain; and remember that while we are working out our own Salvation with Fear and Trembling, God will work in us to will and to do of His own good Pleasure. Let us be so far from depending upon ourselves, as intirely to depend upon the Lord, who will not be wanting to us,. but a present Help in Trouble. Wait upon the Lord, and improve that Measure of Light, and Grace bestowed upon thee, and thou shalt grow as a Tree planted by the Rivers of Water, that bringeth forth Fruit in Season; then thy Leaf shall not wither, and whatsoever thou dost shall prosper. The Dew of Heaven shall be upon thy Root, and thou shalt grow and flourish in the Courts of the Lord. Exercise Self-denial, and take up the Cross of Christ (for *No Cross, No Crown*) Follow Christ the Captain of our Salvation, who was made Perfect through Sufferings. Be not ashamed of the *Cross* of *Christ*, but *Glory* in it, as the Apostle *Paul* did, who said he would Glory in nothing else; Labour to grow in Grace,. and in the Knowledge of our Lord and Saviour Jesus Christ, and to *abound* in all the Fruits of the Spirit, *Love, Joy, Peace, Long-suffering, Goodness, Gentleness, Faith, Meekness and Temperance*; This is to be a Christian indeed, and a true *Jew* or *Israelite, For he is not a* Jew *which is one outwardly, neither is that Circumcision which is outward in the Flesh, but he is a* Jew *which is one inwardly, and Circumcion is that of the Heart, in the Spirit, and not in the Letter, whose Praise is not of Men but of God.* Friends,

Think

Think not that a Superficial and outſide Religion will ſerve you, but you muſt ſhew forth the Virtues of Chriſt and the Power of Godlineſs; then everlaſting Joy will be your Portion. O my Friends, come into the Light, and walk in it as Children of Light, and perſevere to the End, and you ſhall come at laſt to partake of the Inheritance among the Saints in Light, and eat of the Fruit of the Tree of Life which grows in the midſt of the Paradiſe of God. Man was caſt out of Paradiſe becauſe of Tranſgreſſion, How ſhall he come back again, and be reſtored to a State of Felicity? The Lord hath provided a Light and a Leader, the Lord Jeſus Chriſt; Bleſſed are they that follow Him, for he will lead in the Way everlaſting. Bleſſed are they which are reconciled to God, and juſtified by Faith, and have Peace with God, through our Lord Jeſus Chriſt; they know Peace and Aſſurance and Satisfaction in themſelves, *For the Work of Righteouſneſs is Peace, and the Fruit of Righteouſneſs Quietneſs and Aſſurance for ever.* Now that you may come to this full Aſſurance, you muſt firſt know Righteouſneſs, and come to Chriſt for it, who is a Righteous Teacher, who will guide and lead you in the Way of Righteouſneſs, and Holineſs, out of your Wilderneſs State wherein you have wandered from the Lord Jeſus Chriſt, *Who is the Way, the Truth and the Life.* Here is ſomething to enter our Hopes upon, here is a firm Bottom to ſtay upon: I reckon (ſaith the Apoſtle) that I was once alive without the Law, but I am now alive through the quickening Power of the Son of God, who is the Reſurrection and

and the Life. This is experimental Religion, which is pure and undefiled; *To visit the Fatherless and the Widow in their Affliction, and to keep ourselves unspotted from the World.* This is a godly Religion, that takes the Spots out of a Man's Garment, and out of his Heart, and that is a Furnace to refine us, and purge away our Dross; that is as Fullers Soap, to wash out all our Spots. If our Spots are taken away, this will restore our Hearts to God, and render them fit to be his living Temples. Receive Christ into your Hearts, and he will purge away your Dross and reprobate Silver, and make you more pure than the *Gold of Ophir*. They that live the Life they live here by the Faith of the Son of God, they live a pure and heavenly Life; The Men of this World live none of this Life: They seem to receive Christ outwardly, but they reject him inwardly. The *Jews* were cut off, because they would not receive Christ outwardly; then the Ax was laid to the Root of the Tree, and they were cut down as Trees that cumber the Ground, and became a desolate People for their Disobedience; and they that would not receive Christ, they died in their Sins; and our compassionate Redeemer he lamented their miserable Condition, and wept over them, *Matt.* xxiii. 37. *Luke* xix. 41, 42. O Jerusalem, Jerusalem, *thou that killest the Prophets, and stonest them that are sent unto thee! How often would I have gathered thy Children together, even as a Hen gathers her Chickens under her Wings, and ye would not! And when he came near, he beheld the City and wept over it, saying, If thou hadst known, even thou at least, in this thy Day, the*
Things

Things which belong unto thy Peace! But now they are hid from thine Eyes. Thus they rejected Christ the Eternal Son of God, and Light of the World: So those that reject the Testimony of the *Ministers* of Christ that speak to them in Christ's Name, they reject Christ himself: Though Christ speaks not now to you immediately in his own Person, yet he speaks to you instrumentally; and if you reject the Testimony that we bring, when we preach Christ to you, you reject Christ as *Jerusalem* did: What was it that *Jerusalem* did reject? They rejected the Grace and Spirit of Christ, they would not open the Door of their Hearts to receive and entertain Christ in the Day of their Visitation: What did become of them? Their House was left unto them Desolate. *I called* (saith the Lord) *but they would not answer; I offered Salvation to them, but they refused; they would not in their Day know the Things that belong to their Peace, and now they are hidden from their Eyes.*

It is the Desire of my Soul, that none of you may hear that Voice in your Consciences, the Things that belong to thy Peace are now hidden from thine Eyes; thou hast had many Talents given to thee, but thou hast not improved them: This is the Condemnation, that Light is come into the World, but thou hast loved Darkness rather than Light; Thou hast had Grace freely offered to thee, but thou hast refused it, turned from it, or turned it into Wantonness.

The Lord hath given us many Divine Calls and Visitations, and hath promised to be our God, if we would be his People; but after all his Kindness

Kindness to us, He justly complains; *My People would none of me: I am the Lord thy God* (saith He to *Israel* of Old) *that brought thee out of the Land of* Egypt; *Open thy Mouth wide and I will fill it, Enlarge thy Desires, and I will satisfy them; but my People would not hearken to my Voice, and* Israel *would none of me; so I gave up them unto their own Hearts Lust, and they walked in their own Counsels. O! that my People had hearkened unto me, and walked in my Ways; I would have fed them with the Finest of the Wheat, and with Honey out of the Rock should I have satisfied them.*

O my Friends, It is a dangerous Thing for a People that are enlightened by the Spirit of God, to trifle away their precious Time and Seasons of Mercy, the Day of Grace and Salvation: O! Therefore work while it is Day, for the Night cometh wherein there is no working; let us be faithful and turn our Eyes to the Light, and walk in it, and live in Obedience to it: God hath been present with us (my Friends) in the Tribulations, Temptations and Afflictions that have attended us, when we have been ready to say, as *David, I shall one Day fall by the Hands of Saul,* and the Enemy will prevail over us; but God hath wonderfully saved and delivered us, and hath been a Shield and Buckler and a strong Tower to us, and as the Shadow of a great Rock in a weary Land. Let nothing be found alive in us that would divert us, or draw us away from God, who alone can satisfy us, and give us the Desire of our Hearts. If we delight ourselves in Him, let us say unto God, *O Lord, thou art my Portion: Whom have I in Heaven but thee? And there is none upon Earth that I desire besides Thee.* Let us make

make War against every Thing that is contrary to God's holy Nature and Will, and abstain from all Filthiness of Flesh and Spirit, and from all Appearance of Evil.

Have a care that your Adversary the Devil does not prevail over you, be not ignorant of his Devices; he goes about continually like a roaring Lion, seeking whom he may devour.

When the Devil assaulted our Saviour in *Peter*, he said, *Get thee behind me Satan, thou favourest not the Things that be of God.* Examine and try yourselves, whether you have a divine Taste and Relish, and favour the Things of the Spirit? When the Devil presents any alluring or charming Temptation, to seduce you from your Duty to God or your Neighbour, or from your great Concern, the Salvation of your immortal Souls; You know what the Temptation tends to, therefore be stedfast in the Faith; *Resist the Devil, and he will fly from you;* and wait upon God in the Name of Christ, and look up to him, and he will open his divine Hand, and shower down his Blessings upon you, and give you the Upper Springs and the Nether Springs also; God will give Grace and Glory, and no good Thing will he withold from you.

O You *Young Ones!* I have a Travel in my Soul for you! Remember your Creator in the Days of your Youth: Give unto God the Prime and Flower of your Time and Strength; Learn to bear the Yoke betimes: Come to the Yoke of Christ: Take his Yoke upon you; though it may fret thy Neck a little, and cause a little Pain, yet be willing to bear it, and thou wilt find that the

Yoke

Yoke of Chrift is an eafy Yoke, and his Burden a light Burden; and that none of his Commandments are grievous. O my Friends! the Pomp and Pleafure and Glory of this vain World prevails over many, and Thoufands are enfnared by it: But it is better, with *Mofes*, to fuffer Affliction with the People of God, than to enjoy the Pleafures of Sin for a Seafon; and to efteem the Reproach of Chrift, greater Riches than the Treafures of the *Egyptian* Kingdom: For if we fuffer with Chrift here, we fhall reign with him hereafter. The Sacrifices of Old were falted with Salt; If you come to know the divine Salt, the Seafonings of Grace, all that is putrified will be done away, and purged out of your Hearts: All that come to Chrift are feafoned with divine Grace, and they will fhine as Lights in the World; but for thofe that are not in Chrift, nor made new Creatures, they are conformed to this World, and the World will love its own; but what will be the End of thefe? They muft go along with thofe that fhall take their Place on the left Hand of Chrift, and be fentenced to Everlafting Deftruction, from the Prefence of the Lord, and from the Glory of his Power.

You that are Lovers of Pleafures more than Lovers of God, that Love the Vanities of the World, and the Pleafures and Paftimes of it, the Supreme and Righteous Judge of the World will bid you depart from him into Everlafting Fire, prepared for the Devil and his Angels; Wherefore you that are young, remember your Creator in your younger Years; and give up your Hearts to God betimes, and confider what

the

the wife Man faith after all his Experience of the Pleafures and Enjoyments of this World, *Vanity of Vanities, All is Vanity and Vexation of Spirit. Remember now thy Creator in the Day of thy Youth, while thy evil Days come not, nor the Years draw nigh, when thou fhalt fay, I have no Pleafure in them:* while thou art like white Paper, Let God write upon thee, before thou art blotted and ftained with the Vanities and impure Pleafures of this World; Set an high Value on early Piety, Get an Intereft in Chrift Jefus, in your young and tender Years, that as of His Fulnefs, you have received Grace for Grace, you may obey it in all Manner of Converfation; For, *Without Holinefs no Man fhall ever fee the Lord.* Perfevere in Holinefs to the End of your Days, that you may receive the End of your Faith, the Salvation of your Souls; O bleffed are they that take Chrift in all his Offices, for a *King, Prieft* and *Prophet!* For a *King* to *Rule* them with the *Scepter* of his *Grace*, and to fubdue their Enemies by the Might of his Power; as a Prieft, to make Atonement for them, and reconcile them to God, and fave them from Sin and from the Wrath to come; and as a Prophet, to inftruct and teach them, and make them wife to Salvation; Bleffed are they that receive the Truth in the Love of it, and love the Truth as it is in Jefus; there is no Condemnation to them; for they walk not after the Flefh, but after the Spirit. While they wait upon the Lord, they renew their Strength; they fhall never be weary of Well-doing; they fhall *mount up with Wings as Eagles; they fhall run, and not be weary; they fhall walk*

and

and not faint. When the Lord faith to them, *Seek ye my Face;* their Hearts will anfwer, *Thy Face Lord will we seek.* Search the Scriptures to know the Mind and Will of God, and Confult the *Oracle within,* the Word of God in your own Hearts; Whether fhall you, or can you go? You have the Words of Eternal Life, from *Chrift within you the Hope of Glory.* You that have begun in the Spirit, do not end in the Flefh; but refift all Temptations from without, and Corruptions within, and you fhall be more than Conquerors, through Chrift that hath loved you; and you fhall witnefs the fulfilling of that Promife, *Him that overcometh will I make a Pillar in the Temple of my God, and he fhall go no more out; and I will write upon him the Name of my God, and the Name of the City of my God, which is new Jerufalem;* and to *him* (faith Chrift) *that overcometh, will I grant to fit with me in my Throne, even as I also overcame and am fat down with my Father in his Throne, and I will give him a White Stone, and a Name, which none knows but he that hath it.* As in your Parifh Books, there is a Regiftering and a writing down of the Names of all that are born there; So in the Book of Life are written down all the Names of the Children of Light, that are born again, born from Above; and God will remember them, and they will remember his loving Kindnefs, and have it ever before their Eyes, and walk in his Truth.

My Friends, It becomes us to be a *willing People,* to bear the Yoke of Chrift chearfully, and not to be like a Bullock unaccuftomed to the Yoke. *If any draw back* (faith the Lord) *my Soul fhall shall have no Pleasure in him.* Let us be willing both to do and suffer the will of God, and follow Christ the Lamb of God whithersoever he goeth; through Persecutions, Sufferings, and Tribulations, bearing his Reproach, and counting it our Honour to suffer Shame and Dishonour for his Name; and have a Holy Ambition to drink of his Cup, and to be baptised with his Baptism. We read *Luke* xx. 20. that the Mother of *Zebedee*'s Children came to Christ with her two Sons, worshipping him, and desiring a certain Thing of him, and he said unto her, *What wilt thou?* She said unto him, *Grant that these my two Sons may sit, the one on thy Right Hand, and the other on thy Left, in thy Kingdom: But Jesus answered and said, Ye know not what ye ask? Are ye able to drink of the Cup that I drink of? And to be baptized with the Baptism that I am Baptized with? They say unto him, We are able.* And our Saviour said unto them, *Ye shall drink indeed of my Cup, and be baptised with the Baptism that I am bap'ised with; but to sit on my Right Hand, and on my Left, is not mine to give; but it shall be given to them, for whom it is prepared of my Father.* What is this Baptism? It is Self-denial, and taking up the *Cross* of *Christ*; and to be willing to part with all for his Sake: To stand at a Distance from the World, and to be weaned from the Enjoyments of it, and to let Christ have the Command and Government of our Hearts, Wills, and Affections.

My Friends, let us so live, as we shall wish we had done, when we come to die: 2 Cor. v. 10, 11, *For we must all appear before the Judgment Seat of Christ, that every one may receive the Things done*

done in his Body, according to that which he hath done, whether it be good or bad: Knowing therefore the Terror of the Lord, we perfuade Men: O bleſſed are they that turn from the Evil of their Ways, and fo hear that their Souls may live; *Obedience is better than Sacrifice; and to hearken, than the Fat of Rams:* Bleſſed are they that ponder, and weigh, and confider what the Lord's Prophets and Meſſengers ſpeak and declare unto them, that are found in a Way of Obedience, and live up to what they know, they ſhall at laſt lay down their Heads in Peace; *For bleſſed are the Dead that die in the Lord, they reſt from their Labours, and their works will follow them.*

O Friends, Come unto Chriſt that you may have Life, and have it abundantly: He is the living Fountain that God hath vouchſafed to open to us, even the Fountain of living Water, for the Refreſhment of thirſty Souls; and the Bread that comes down from Heaven, for filling and ſatisfying the hungry Soul. Bleſſed are they that know Chriſt to be their Shepherd, and hear his Voice, and follow him, who will go before them as their Light and Leader, and give them *Eternal Life.* They ſhall receive from him in this Life Food convenient; he will make them lie down in *Green Paſtures,* and lead them by the ſtill Waters, and he will prepare a Table before them in the midſt of their Enemies, and ſatisfy them as with Marrow and Fatneſs, and make them triumph in his Love and Praiſe. Let us travel on in the Path of Life, in the ways of Righteouſneſs, without fainting, and labour to anſwer the great End of our Creation, and the Deſign of God's
Love

Love in our Redemption, and let us live as Witnesses for God in our own Generation. But some may say, What do we witness? I witness to God's Judgment for my Sin, and to his Mercy in forgiving my Sin, and to his good Spirit visiting my Soul, and sanctifying me, and making me free from the Law of Sin and Death; and I witness (may a sincere and humble Soul say) a Freedom and Deliverance from the Bondage of Corruption, and Power and Victory over the World, and the Flesh, and the Devil, the grand Enemy of my Salvation. O that you may all Experience these great Things in your own Souls! Then Christ will say unto every one of you, *Well done good and faithful Servant, Thou hast been faithful in a little, I will make thee Ruler over much.* The Joy of the Lord shall enter now into thee, and thou shalt hereafter enter into the Joy of thy Lord; thou shalt then behold his Face in Righteousness, and be eternally satisfied with his Likeness: *In whose Presence is Fulness of Joy, and at whose Right Hand are Pleasures for Evermore.*

THE
HEAVENLY RACE.

A SERMON PREACHED AT THE QUAKER's MEETING-HOUSE IN GRACE-CHURCH-STREET, LONDON, JANUARY 16. 1694.

BY WILLIAM PENN.

THE *Life* of *Man* and *Woman* is compared unto a *Race*, that is to be *run*; and unto a *Post*, that makes *haste*: And our daily Experience confirms, what the Holy Ghost hath lively set forth and expressed to us by the Holy Men of God, in several Ages and Generations. We are all of us, that are here this Day, running our natural *Race*; Our *Time* is spending on, and we are every Day a Step nearer to the Grave. God requires, that we will every Day draw nigh to him: Blessed are all those, that are every Day a Step nearer to *God*, as well as a Step nearer to the *Grave*, and to Eternity! If you draw nigh to God, he will draw nigh to you, and turn every one of you from your Iniquities, and keep you from returning to Folly.

Friends, Of ourselves we can do nothing, except the Lord be present with us, and strengthen and uphold us: Blessed are those, that live in an humble Sense of their own Insufficiency, and are in a true *Poverty* of *Spirit*, and as the Light of every Morning appears, are waiting upon God,

as

as a Watch-man waits for the Morning. I say *Wait* upon Him, for the lifting up of the Light of his Countenance: *They that wait upon the Lord, shall renew their Strength; they shall mount up with Wings as Eagles; they shall run, and not be weary; they shall walk and not* wax *faint,* while they walk in the Way of Holiness, that leads to Eternal Blessedness.

All those, who are Faithful, and Approved of God at this Day, they will not want the *Presence* of the *Lord* with them, and his Hand to uphold them: He will be a God nigh at Hand to all, that are *true Travellers* with their Faces *Zion-*ward. All that are *Travellers* to a blessed Eternity, to that World that shall never have an End: These shall never want the divine Presence of the Lord Jesus Christ, the *Son* of *God*; concerning whom God saith, *I will give Him for a Light and a Leader, a King and Lawgiver.* Now all you, who obey his Voice, and come under his Holy Conduct and Teaching, and have denied yourselves, and resolved to take up his *Cross*, and follow him, and will not be ashamed of his *Cross*, but *Glory* in it; I testify to you from the Lord, That *God is with you,* and will be with you if faithful. He is such a Leader, as will lead you in the *Way* of *Righteousness,* and in the midst of the *Paths* of *Judgment*; He will fill your Treasures, and make you to inherit Substance.

O my Friends! You cannot imagine, what Peace and Joy, and Divine Consolation, there is in such a good State and Condition, when you have the *Witness* within yourselves, that you give up your Hearts to *God!* God will be always present with you, and withhold no good Thing
from

from you; This is my Testimony to you this Day. O Gird up the Loins of your Minds; be sober and Hope to the End. Take heed to your Ways, and turn your Feet to *God's* Testimonies, while you are in your heavenly Race; turn neither to the *Right Hand*, nor to the *Left*, but so *Run*, that you may *Obtain*. There is a *Running*, where People may miss the *Prize* and fall short; and there is a *Running* where they may obtain the Crown. *Let us therefore lay aside every Weight, and the Sin that doth easily beset us; and run with Patience that Race that is set before us, looking unto Jesus, the Author and Finisher of our Faith; who for the Joy that was set before him, endured the Cross, and despised the Shame.* Let us have an Eye to *Christ* the great *Captain of our Salvation*, and we shall be sensible of his living Presence, and feel his Everlasting Arms, to uphold us. If we press forward, and strive to enter in at the *strait Gate*, we shall receive the Recompence of Reward, after all our *Sufferings, Afflictions, Poverty, Troubles, Tribulations, Scoffings, Cruel Mockings, Reproach, Buffetings, Losses* and *Crosses, and Persecutions*, that we have undergone in this World for Christ's Sake. O let none of us be dejected or discouraged, but wait for the Salvation of God: Take no thought for the *Morrow*, let the *Morrow* take thought for the Things of itself: Sufficient unto the Day is the Evil thereof. Let your *Affections* be set upon Things above, and not carried after perishing Things here below: When *Temptations* do assault you, they shall not prevail; for you shall experience with the Apostle *Paul,* That *the Grace of God will be sufficient for you*

you. Blessed be the *Name* of the *Lord* for ever, who hath engaged by Promise to support and fortify his People in the *Hour* of *Temptation*. While we live in this World, *Trials* and *Troubles*, *Temptations*, and *Tribulations* will attend us; we shall not be out of the Reach of them on this Side the Grave. *Your Adversary the Devil goes about like a roaring Lion, continually seeking whom he may devour; whom resist, being stedfast in Faith*; and you shall be able to quench all the fiery Darts of the *Devil*, and be more than Conquerors through Christ that hath loved you.

And when you come to the New *Jerusalem*, into the strong City of God, you shall sing Songs of Praise and Thanksgiving to your great *Deliverer*, and have *Salvation* for Walls and Bulwarks round about you, and triumph in his Praise, who hath dealt bountifully with you, and by his Mighty Arm hath done wonderful Things for you, and remembred you in your low Estate; because his *Mercy* endureth for ever.

Such was the Infidelity, Rebellion, and Ingratitude of *Israel* of old, while they were in the Wilderness, *fed with Quails and Manna from, Heaven*, Psa. cv. 15. and supplied with *Water out of the Rock*, by a miraculous Providence, yet they murmured against the Lord, and they entered not into the good Land, because of their *Unbelief*: Take heed of shutting yourselves out of the Cœlestial *Canaan* by your *Unbelief* and *Disobedience*. As in your *Natural Race* you are every Day one Step nearer the Grave, so in your *Spiritual Race*, be every Day advancing in your Progress towards a blessed Eternity; That when you

come

come to die, and leave this World, you may live Eternally, and be for ever with the Lord. O live now as an experienced and concerned People, that you may be of the Number of the *Wife Virgins*, who have Oil in their Lamps and in their Vessels; and that you may in all Approaches to God be found *Spiritual Worshippers*, and offer up to Him a pure Offering, that your *Prayers* may be as Incense and Sweet Odours, most acceptable to Him through the Intercession of the Lord *Jesus Christ*, the great Mediator, who is the King of Saints. Submit to his Sceptre and Government, as an obedient and willing People, that you nay take Sanctuary in His mighty Name; who is called *Jesus*, the *Mighty Saviour*, who will save his People from their Sins and from the Wrath to come.

When you are concerned deeply about your Spiritual and *Eternal State*, and cry out, *What shall we do to be saved?* And when you are humbled and afflicted for your Sins, he will deal tenderly with you, and have Compassion on you: For *he will not break the bruised Reed, nor quench the smoaking Flax;* He shall bring forth Judgment unto Truth. But many are stopt in the Way, because *Judgment* hath not its perfect Work: They are not yet humbled under the mighty Hand of God, and will not submit to the Lord *Jesus Christ*, but say obstinately, *We will not have this Man to reign over us.* But our Lord JESUS, the Lion of the Tribe of *Judah*, saith concerning such, *But these mine Enemies, that will not that I should reign over them, bring hither, and slay them before me.* Mat. xix. 27.

O *Friends*,

O Friends, Let us all be a willing People, and take *Christ* for our *Saviour* and *Sovereign,* who is our Rightful Lord; *Who died* (faith the Apostle) *and revived, and rose again, that he might be Lord both of the Dead and Living.* Let us live to Christ, that died for us; Live to him here, and we shall live with him for ever. Let our Souls praise the Lord, and all that is within us bless his holy Name, that hath sent his Son from Heaven to seek and to save us that were lost, and to redeem us from all Iniquity, that we might be a peculiar People, *zealous of good Works.* Blessed be God, who daily loadeth us with his *Benefits* and *Blessings!* And blessed be Christ, our Redeemer, the Lord of Life, who hath invited us to come to him, that we might have Life; that we may eat of the Fruit of the Tree of Life, whose Leaves are for the Healing of the Nations: That we may sit under his shadow with great Delight, and his *Fruit* will be sweet unto our Taste. Our Lord *Jesus* will feed us with Heavenly *Manna,* and with *Honey* out of the *Rock* of our *Salvation,* and the true and living *Bread,* that came down from Heaven: He will make us a *Feast of fat Things, and with Wine on the Lees well refined.* O remember the loving Kindness of God, let it ever be before your Eyes, that you may walk in his Truth, as the Royal *Psalmist* speaks. And when the *Meeting* is over, keep your Watch, and let not the spirit of the World, nor the Prince of the Power of the Air, that rules in the Children of Disobedience, hinder the good Seed (the Word) from taking Root; and bringing forth *Fruit,* that may abound to God's Eternal Glory and Praise, and your Everlasting Consolation.

O Friends,

O Friends, Live for Heaven and Eternity, and labour abundantly in the Work of the Lord; and you shall know to your Joy and Comfort, that your Labour shall not be in Vain. Do you now follow your Works while you live, and your Works shall follow you, when you die: Rev. xiii. 7. *Blessed are the Dead that die in the Lord, for they shall rest from their labours, and their Works follow them.* I would not have you think, that I put you upon any depending upon your own (best) *Works*; For if we do any *good Work*, it is by the help and Assistance of the *Spirit of Christ,* by whose Power alone we are enabled to do it. It is by the *Strength and Power of Christ Jesus,* in whom we believe: It is by that Strength and Power, that we derive from Him, that we are kept *faithful* to the *Death,* that we may obtain the *Crown* of *Life.* It is by *Christ* alone, the Great *Captain* of our *Salvation,* that we must conquer our Spiritual Enemies, resist the *Devil,* and overcome the World, and be more than Conquerors; That persevering in Holiness to the End of our Days, we may say with the Apostle *Paul,* when we come to die, *I have fought a good Fight, I have finished my Course, I have kept the Faith; Henceforth is laid up for me a Crown of Righteousness, which the Lord, the righteous Judge, shall give me at that Day; and not to me only, but unto all them also, that love his Appearing.*

Therefore I beseech you all, to give all Diligence, to make your *Calling* and *Election* sure, and so run in your *Heavenly Race,* as to press forward, towards the Mark of the High Calling of God in *Christ Jesus,* that you may obtain Life Eternal.

Eternal. *The Grace of God, that bringeth Salvation, hath appeared to all Men; and God so loved the World, that he gave his only begotten Son, that whosoever believeth in him, should not perish, but have Everlasting Life.* And the Invitation is made to all ; *Look unto me, and be ye saved all ye Ends of the Earth.* Salvation is offered to all, and the Means of obtaining it, is by *Faith in Christ Jesus,* the dear and blessed *Son of God,* who was born of the Virgin *Mary,* and took our Nature, as the Son of *David* and the Seed of *Abraham*; As he was made *Man,* he was a confinable Being ; But he is also both *God* and *Man,* so he is Infinite and Eternal, God over all, blessed for ever ! Come then to Christ, that you may have Life and Quickening, vital Influence from him, and of his Fullness receive Grace for Grace : Come to the *Blood of Jesus,* that purifying *Fountain,* to wash you from all your Sins, and wipe off all your old Scores. Christ is made not only Wisdom and Righteousness, but Sanctification and Redemption to us : *We are justified freely by the* Grace of God, *through the Redemption, that is in Jesus Christ.*

Walk in Love (faith the Apostle) *as Christ also hath loved us, and given himself for us an Offering and a Sacrifice to God for a sweet smelling Savour.* God offers Salvation to us in Christ, the *Second Adam,* who only can redeem us from that Bondage and Misery, which the *first Adam* by his Fall and Apostacy brought on all Mankind.

Christ is the only Saviour of Sinners, and the Author of Eternal Salvation to all them that believe in him and obey him. This is the Generation of them that seek the Lord, they believe in the

the Lord Jesus Christ, who came from Heaven to shew them the Way thither, and came to seek and save them that were lost. *Lift up your Heads, O ye Gates, and be ye lift up, ye Everlasting Doors, and the King of Glory shall come in: Who is this King of Glory? The Lord strong and mighty, the Lord mighty in Battle*; the Lord *Jesus Christ*, who is mighty to save our Souls, and to subue all the Enemies of our Salvation.

Now unto him that hath loved us, and washed us from our Sins in his own Blood, and hath made us Kings and Priests unto God and his Father, To whom be Glory and Dominion, for ever and ever.
Amen.

THE
DYING COUNSEL
OF THE
WONDERFUL COUNSELLOR:

A SERMON PREACHED AT THE QUAKER'S MEETING-HOUSE IN DEVONSHIRE-HOUSE, LONDON, JANUARY 20. 1694.

BY WILLAAM PENN.

IT was the bleffed Encouragement that our Lord Jefus Chrift gave to his Difciples, and all his Followers (when he took on him the Nature of Man, and was made Flefh, and dwelt amongft us) and therein to all the Sons and Daughters of Men, who fhould follow him through the many and great Tribulations, and give up their Names and Hearts to him, to be Witneffes of his Truth, and of that holy Teftimony which he fhould communicate to them near his *Farewell,* and a little before his being offered up, *Let not your Hearts be troubled; ye believe in God, believe alfo in me: In my Father's Houfe are many Manfions; If it were not fo, I would have told you; I go to prepare a Place for you, and I will come again and receive you unto myfelf, that where I am, there you may be alfo:* Now my *Friends,* Thefe Manfions they are the Recompences of Reward that are set in the View of the Righteous, and promised of God by Christ Jesus. These many *Mansions* are the manifold Rewards, Diversities of Rewards, that refer to the Diversity of States, and Conditions and Persons, unto whom these many Mansions do belong. As all are not of the same Stature and Growth, neither are all these Mansions of the same Degree of Glory and Felicity. *There is one Glory of the Sun, another Glory of the Moon, another Glory of the Stars; for one Star differs from another Star in Glory;* Yet all these Stars shine with a Lustre and Glory, and the least Star hath a Beauty and Excellency in it; and so the least of these many Mansions hath a marvellous Light and Glory in it. This refers to the State of every Man and Woman here below. All Members are not the Hand, all are not the Head, but every Member of the Body hath its Service, and will have its Reward. This is that which did spring up in my Soul this Morning, as I sat here among you. O that all here present may become the living Members of Christ Jesus our blessed Head, and live the Life they live in the Body, by the Faith of the Son of God. He that made us, knows our Frame; He that created us, and formed and fashioned us after his own Image, and gave us Powers and Faculties to glorify and serve him, that we may come to enjoy him for ever, he requires of no Man or Woman more than he hath given them Power and Ability to perform. It concerneth us all therefore to live in the Exercise of that divine Gift, and Grace, and Ability which our Lord Jesus Christ hath distributed and communicated to eve-

ry

ry Member of his Body, that we may come to shine as *Stars* in the Firmament of Glory. We should do good in our several Places and Stations, according to our different Powers and Capacities. And as every Member is by the Circulation of Blood made useful and beneficial in the natural Body, so the *Divine Life and Blood of the Son of God circulates through his whole Myſtical Body,* and reaches Life to every living Member. Here is no Obſtruction through Unfaithfulneſs, or Inordinate Love of the World, or any Temptation from without us, or Corruption from within us. Here is a free Channel, here is an open Paſſage for Life and quickening Influences from Chriſt our Glorious *Head,* to all his Members. There is in Chriſt (in whom the Fulneſs of the God-Head dwells bodily) a River, whoſe Streams make glad the *City* of *God:* A *Fountain* to supply and refreſh the whole Generation of the Righteous, *That deſire to be found in him* (as the Apoſtle ſpeaks) *not having their own Righteouſneſs, but cloathed with the* Robe *of his Righteouſneſs, which is the* Garment *of* Salvation. Therefore wait this Day, *My dear Friends,* to have your Hearts filled with the *Love* and *Life* of the Son of God, that you may appear with Joy at his *Tribunal,* where all Mankind muſt appear, and every one give an Account of what he hath done in the Body, whether it be Good or Evil. Let every one of you be careful to live according to what you know, and improve the *Talents* that God hath given you, and you ſhall find that in keeping his Commandments, there is great Reward, and that God is good to *Iſrael,* to them that are of a clean Heart.

G 2 Had

Had not the Lord been on our Side, may *Ifrael* fay; Had not the Lord been on our Side when Men rofe up againft us, may we fay, they had fwallowed us up, and the Temptations of the Devil would have prevailed over us, and we had fallen long ago. It is not we that have ftood firm in Times of Trial and Trouble, but it is the Lord that hath ftood by us, and made us to ftand: And the Love of God to his People now, is as great as ever it was: *His Arm is not fhortened that it cannot fave, nor his Ear heavy that it cannot hear;* Therefore travel on and faint not, and you fhall come with Joy to the End of your *Journey,* and you fhall be fatisfied with the *Fatnefs* of God's *Houfe,* and fay with the Pfalmift, *Bleffed are they that dwell in thy Houfe, they fhall be ftill praifing thee.* It is the Faithful and Sincere that fhall dwell in the Houfe of the Lord for ever, and enter into his Everlafting Kingdom. O My Friends, live as a People bowed down in the Prefence of the Great and Holy God, and walk humbly with him: Be humbled under his mighty Hand, and you fhall be exalted in due Time.

The God of Heaven hath vifited your Souls with his Divine Power and Grace, and given you a refrefhing Senfe of his Love, that you may perceive and feel a daily renewing of your Strength. O wait upon the Lord for his Divine Power to enable you to Conquer the Power of Satan, that you may go on conquering and to conquer, till you come to the New *Jerufalem,* the *City* of God and Land of Peace and Reft. Beware of *Idolatry!* Bow not down to the Work of your own Hands:
For

For tho' you may not be guilty of *Gross Idolatry*, yet there is a secret, and more hidden *Idolatry*, that too many are guilty of, Who set their Hearts and Affections on low and earthly Things: This sticks but too near to many. Let the Word of Exhortation of the Apostle enter into your Hearts; *Little Children keep yourselves from* Idols. Let this be the Cry of your *Souls*, Lord preserve and keep me this Day, every Day and to the End of my Days, that I may not only be convinced of the Truth, but really converted to it, and walk in the Truth and persevere therein to the End, that I may be saved. Remember *Lot*'s Wife; Look not back to *Sodom: Walk in the Light as Children of Light*, with your Faces *Sion*-Ward; and rejoice in hope of the Glory of God. Ye *were sometime Darkness, but now (saith the Apostle) Ye are Light in the Lord.* O shine as *Stars* in the midst of a crooked and perverse Generation. Shine in the Beauties of Holiness, and walk in the Light of Christ, the Son of Righteousness, who was given for a Light to lighten the Gentiles, and to be the Glory of his People *Israel*. He shall be the Desire of all Nations; the mighty Saviour, upon whom God hath laid Help. Believe in him, cleave to him, and follow him, and you shall be saved, both from your Sins, and from the Wrath to come. *God is Light* (saith the Apostle *John*) *in him is no Darkness at all*; *If we walk in the Light as he is in the Light, then we shall have Fellowship one with another, and the Blood of Jesus Christ his Son cleanseth us from all Sin*; We know him to be the true *Rock* and the Foundation of God, which standeth sure, and which will stand sure, in stormy my and tempestuous Times: Blessed are they that build upon this Foundation which God hath laid.

Blessed be God, which hath opened your Eyes, and given you to see this sure Foundation, which we must build all our Hopes of Salvation upon: And not upon any other Foundation whatsoever. Not upon Mens Arts, and Parts, and human Acquirements. O the unsearchable Riches of Christ! That we may, and are only to covet and seek after; then we shall inherit Substance indeed, and may say of a Truth, The Lord is good unto his People; He will satisfy them with his loving Kindness, which is better than Life, and surround them with his Almighty Arm, and be unto them as the Shadow of a great *Rock* in a weary *Land*. Be not discouraged, notwithstanding the furious and impetuous Assaults of your spiritual Enemies; when God is pleased to arise for your Help, your Enemies shall be scattered. *In the World* (saith our Saviour) *Ye shall have Trouble, but in Me ye shall have Peace; Be of good Cheer I have overcome the World.* Our Lord Jesus Christ conquered and triumphed over the World, and over Principalities and Powers, and *Death* and *Hell*, and we shall overcome through him that hath loved us; His Grace will be sufficient for us; Let us wait for his Salvation, and in order to it, wait to know, and then do his Mind and Will, and so redeem our Time, and double our Diligence, that we may improve our Talents, and give up our Account with Joy. And then if we are under Doubts and Fears, we may say with *David, Why art thou cast down, O my Soul, and why art thou disquieted within me? Hope thou in God, for I shall*

I shall yet praise him, for the Help of his Countenance. God is pleased to Exercise his People many Times with divers Troubles, Trials, and Afflictions, to wean them from this World, and from an inordinate Love to the Pleasures and Enjoyment of it, that their Minds may not be drawn away by the Things that are seen, which are temporal, from the Things that are not seen, which are Eternal. Let us take straight Steps towards the Glory that shall be revealed; that as every Day we are a Step nearer the Grave, we may be also a Step nearer to a blessed Eternity. It was the Voice of *Moses the Man of God*, and that which he had in Charge from Heaven concerning the Children of *Israel*, in their March towards *Canaan*, say unto the People, Go forward: There is a good Land before you; a Land flowing with *Milk* and *Honey*. The Lord was with them and wrought great Things for them, and he hath also wrought great Things for us. Let us all press therefore forward towards the Mark of the high Calling of God in Christ Jesus, till we come to that *City* that hath Foundations, whose Builder and Maker is God; and that Kingdom that cannot be shaken, which God hath prepared for them that love Him. O that every one of you, upon a serious Examination of yourselves, may find yourselves in a good State and Condition towards God; Travelling through the Wilderness of this World, your Eyes upon Heaven. Let your Prayers and strong Cries be to the Lord for his Help; for we are not sufficient of ourselves for any good Word or Work. It is his Almighty Arm and Power only that can enable us to overcome our spiritual

tual Enemies, and to work out our own Salvation with Fear and Trembling; yea and to work in us, both to will and to do of his own good Pleasure. And pray let us, with *Moses*, chuse rather to suffer Afflictions with the People of God, than to enjoy the Pleasures of Sin for a Season: And turn our Backs upon this World, and the Glory of it; and live so, as seeing him that is invisible. Let us follow them, who, thro' Faith and Patience have inherited the Promises. There are Thousands of faithful Witnesses gathered to their Eternal Rest; Let us follow the Foot-steps of the Flock; that little Flock, for which God hath prepared a Kingdom. Take a Prospect of Heaven by the Eye of Faith, in the Light of Christ Jesus; and behold the Glory of God shining upon you in the Face of Jesus Christ. Suffer not your Hearts to cleave to this World, nor to any Pleasure or Enjoyment in it, that may be a Snare and Temptation to draw your Minds and Affections from the *Giver to the Gift*. Live a Self-denying Life: Keep your Dominion, you that have it, over that which hath had Dominion over you, and then you may say, thy Kingdom's come, and thy Will is done, on Earth as it is in Heaven. Then the Power of Sin shall be subdued in your Souls, and the Body of Sin, and Death shall be destroyed; and as you have had cause to cry out, with the Apostle, *O wretched man that I am, who shall deliver me from the Body of Sin and Death!* So each of you will be able to rejoice, and say with him, I thank God through Jesus Christ our Lord, I am made free from the Law of Sin and Death. And my Friends, when the Mountain of the Lord's

Lord's House shall be set a Top of all the Mountains, then shall you rejoice and praise his Holy Name.

O that the Nations round about might come to the saving Knowledge of God and Jesus Christ, which is Life Eternal. O look for the Appearance and Manifestation of the Son of God in your Hearts, then you will admire and adore the Mercy, Justice, Holiness, Goodness, Patience, and Long-suffering of God, which will lead you to Repentance, then you will cry out and say God is Just, God is Merciful, God is Holy, and abundant in Goodness and Truth; He hath made us sensible of the Riches of his Goodness, and of his Forbearance, Patience, and Long-suffering: I will bless and praise his Holy, Great and Excellent Name; and say, *Whom have I in Heaven but thee? And there is none upon Earth that I desire in Comparison of thee. In thy Favour is Life, and thy loving Kindness is better than Life,* and that, which I esteem above all Things on the Face of the Earth. O Friends, be you thankful to God for the Manifestation of his Love and Mercy to you!

Take Heed of an ungrateful Spirit. Trust in the Lord and he will deliver you, and wound the hairy Scalp of your Enemies. Many have outlived their youthful Greenness, and that Tenderness they had when God first awakened them to consider their Ways, and to seek after him with their whole Heart. I *Remember,* saith the Lord by *Jeremiah, the Kindness of thy Youth, and the Day of thy Espousals.* God will remember you, if you remember his loving Kindness, and have it ever before your Eyes, and walk in his Truth. When there was nothing but Darkness in *Egypt*, there was Light in *Goshen*, *We* (faith the Apostle) *were sometimes Darkness, but now we are Light in the Lord:* Let us walk then as Children of the Light, and hate the Works of Darkness.

We that are made living Witnesses of the Power, and Wisdom, and Goodness of God, Let us sink down into Self-abasement, and Humility, and we shall feel the living Openings of the Spirit of Truth in our own Hearts, and receive with Meekness that ingrafted Word, in which is Light and Life, that is able to save our Souls; and submit to the Authority of God therein; that the Word of Christ may dwell richly in us, and become the Power of God to our Salvation.

Now the God of Peace which brought again from the Dead our Lord Jesus Christ, the Great Shepherd of his Sheep, through the Blood of the Everlasting Covenant, Make you Perfect in every Good Work, to do his Will; Working in you that which is well pleasing in his Sight, to whom be Glory, Praise, and Thanksgiving, who alone is worthy, who is God over all, blessed for ever and ever. Amen.

THE GREAT DESIGN OF CHRISTIANITY.

A SERMON PREACHED AT THE QUAKER'S MEETING-HOUSE IN WHEELERS-STREET, LONDON, JANUARY 27. 1694.

BY WILLIAM PENN.

THE Great End for which God hath in all Ages and Generations vifited the Sons and Daughters of Men, hath been to bring them home to himfelf; to make Man and Woman fenfible of that Duty which they owe to *God*, to their *Neighbours* and to *Themfelves*. And in order to effect this, great hath been God's Love, and manifold have been his Mercies: He hath not taken Man at his Word, neither would he be put off at once, twice, or thrice, but repeated have been the Vifitations of God, and the Calls of God, in every Age and Generation of the World, according to the various Adminiftrations thereof; Yea, the Lord hath waited to be good and gracious to Mankind from the beginning.

And now, my Friends, we have not only the Teftimony of the Holy Records of the Scriptures of Truth, but we have our own Experience to exalt God's love by: We in our Day, We Mankind

kind in our age and Generation; we can say that God is good, we can say that God is a long-suffering God, and that God is a God of Patience, and that he is a God of Mercy, and that he hath waited long to be gracious to us, or we had been cut off long ago, and taken out of the Land of the Living. I would have all those that have not laid hold of the Long-suffering of *God*, but have made light of it, not do so any longer, but that the long-suffering of God might lead them to Repentance, and bring Salvation to them; that they would lay hold of the Time and blessed Opportunities which God giveth them, and hearken to the Voice of the Charmer, and give Ear to the Voice of God, and seek the Lord while he may be found, and call upon him while he is near to hear them, while he is near to help them, while he is near to save them. This is the Experience we have had, the Lord hath visited us and touched us, and made us sensible of his love and kindness to us, in his gathering of us; and that he hath made us nigh, that were afar off; and that those that are not convinced, may be made sensible of their Sin; and those that are Convinced, may be Converted; and those that are Converted, may persevere to the End, and receive the End of their Faith, the Salvation of their Souls, is our Travail.

Let all that are really convinced of the Evil of their Ways and Doings, of their Wantonness, Worldliness, Malice and Bitterness, Strife and Envyings, and Animosities, and those things that the Light of Christ in their own Consciences condemn them for; Let all that are in such a state of Conviction, turn from that Evil they are convinced of.

But

But here is the Sin, and Misery, and Ruin of many Men and Women, they flatter themselves into Hell, with their false hopes of Heaven: They hope to live Eternally happy by the Death of Christ, and yet they will not leave one Sin for the love of Christ; so that Sin and death reign over them. They that will not mortify Sin, and die to Sin here, must die for their Sins hereafter. It is only Unpardoned Sin that will sink Men into Perdition. They that have a mournful sense of Sin, and a true Contrition for it, they will humble themselves under the mighty hand of God, who will exalt them in due time. They breathe forth holy Desires, and lift up their Hearts to God, and say, *Lord, I am as Clay in the hands of the Potter, O fashion and shape me, that I may be an honourable Vessel in thy House, that I may be fit to glorify thee, and shew forth thy Praise: Blessed are they that dwell in thy House, for they will be still praising thee; they offer praise, and glorify thee here for a short time, and thou wilt glorify them to Eternity.* God called *Abraham*, the Father of the Faithful, out of his own Land, a Land of Idolatry; he obeyed the Voice of God, went into a strange Country and followed the Lord, *not knowing whither he went:* So God calls the Sons and Daughters of Men out of their Sin and Transgression, that they may come to a Land that flows with Milk and Honey; that after all their wearisome Labours and Travels, through the Wilderness of this World, they might come to an *Everlasting Rest*, and obtain *Salvation* for their Immortal Souls. They that come to be convinced of the Evil of their Ways, and turn from them, that bitterly bewail their Sins,

Sins, and lament and mourn for their Trangreffions, and turn to the Lord with all their Hearts; it may be said concerning such, These have learned that Divine *Arithmetick*, of Numbering their Days, and applying their Hearts to true Wisdom: these are the Persons that take heed to their Ways, and turn their feet to God's Testimonies. They take more care, and are more concerned for their Souls, than for all the perishing things of this World. Such a one will say, My Soul is more worth than ten Thousand Worlds: *What will it profit me to gain the whole World, and lose mine own Soul? Or what shall I give in exchange for my Soul?* What is this World but an empty Bubble, a shadow that flies away? All its Glittering Profits, and Charming Pleasures, and Delusory Honours, that appear great to a Carnal Eye, how quickly do they Vanish and Disappear, and afford no true Satisfaction to them that admire them, and pursue after them? *Vanity of Vanities* (saith the Wisest of Men) *Vanity of Vanities, all is Vanity, and Vexation of Spirit!* But wordly-minded Men, that set their Hearts upon this World, they are not for these holy Reflections; but the truly convinced Men and Women, that are touched with a deep sense of their Misery, and of their own erring and straying, and wandering from God's holy Ways, that fear to sin and provoke the Lord, and stir up the Indignation of the Almighty, they love to reflect upon themselves, and to consider their Ways, and turn to the Lord, and to set their Faces *Sion*-Ward: I say to all such Persons, Travel on, the Lord hath been Gracious to you.

O improve

O improve your precious time! You know not how few Days you have yet remaining to run your great Race in. *To Day, while it is called to Day, if you will hear the Voice of God, harden not your hearts, as in the Provocation, in the Day of Temptation in the Wildernefs.* Let none of you be carelefs and flack, but let every one of you confider your latter end, confider how far you have done the Work of God, and whether you have been working out your own Salvation with fear and trembling, and give all Diligence to make your Calling and Election fure ; that when you come to lay down your Heads, it may be as Conquerors that have fought the good Fight, and overcome the Enemy of your Souls.

O Friends, we have a great and fubtle Enemy: If we be fecure, and keep not our Watch, he will furprife us and overcome us ; but if we refift him, and fight againft him, we fhall overcome him through Chrift that hath loved us. *O wretched Man that I am* (faith the Apoftle) *who fhall deliver me ? I thank God, through Jefus Chrift our Lord*; He will deliver me from this great *Goliah*, that hath led me captive at his will. It is Chrift that ftands at the Door of my Heart and knocks, and bids me open to him that will be my Deliverer : It is he of whom *David* was a Type, he will deliver me, and enable me to overcome that *Goliah*, that Grand Enemy of my Soul. When the Sons of *Jeffe* came before *Samuel*, one of whom God had appointed him to anoint King over *Ifrael*, the Lord faid to *Samuel, Look not on his Countenance, or on the height of his Stature, becaufe I have refufed him ; for the Lord feeth not as Man feeth : for*

Man

Man looketh on the outward appearance, but the Lord looketh on the Heart: And Jesse, *made Seven of his Sons to pass before* Samuel, *and he said to* Jesse, *The Lord hath not chosen these: Then he sent and brought* David, *his youngest Son, a Keeper of Sheep, And He was Anointed King.* He was little in Stature, and Ruddy, and withal of *Beautiful* Countenance and Complexion; yet was strong in Heart, and of great Courage; of a Wise and Heavenly Mind, that lived in the fear of the Lord, and also a Man after God's own Heart. When he came to fight *Goliah,* that Monstrous Giant, that defied the Armies of the Living God, King *Saul* armed young *David* with his own Armour, and put an Helmet of Brass upon his Head, and also put on him a Coat of Mail, and he girded his Sword upon his Armour. And *David* put them off him, and said to *Saul, I cannot go with these, for I have not proved them.* David fights *Goliah* after his own manner, out of the road of the Mighty, and of the Great Ones of the Earth: He *took only his Staff in his hand, and chose him Five smooth Stones out of the Brook, and put them in a Shepherd's Bag, and his Sling was in his hand, and he drew near to the Philistine: And when* Goliah *saw* David, *he despised him, for he was but a Youth, and ruddy, and of a fair Countenance: Then said* David *to the* Philistine, *Thou comest to me with a Sword and a Spear, and with a Shield; but I come to thee* IN THE NAME OF THE LORD OF HOSTS, *whom thou hast defied. This Day will the Lord deliver thee into my hand: And* David *put his hand in his Bag, and took thence a Stone and slang it, and smote the Philistine in the Forehead, and the stone sunk into his Forehead, he fell upon his* Face

Face to the Earth; So David *prevailed over* Goliah, *with a Sling and a Stone, and smote him, and slew him; but there was no Sword in the hand of* David. Thus he conquered that great Giant, though he was little and despised. So our Lord Jesus Christ (of whom *David* was a Type) when he came into the World, he was rejected and despised of Men; but notwithstanding, there were many that beheld his Glory, as the Glory of the only begotten of the Father, full of Grace and Truth.

My Friends, It's Christ that hath Conquered the Devil, that *Goliah* and great Enemy of our Souls: He hath spoiled Principalities and Powers, and overcome Death, and Hell, and all the Powers of Darkness: We also obtain the Victory and are made more than Conquerors, through the Lord Jesus Christ, the great Captain of our Salvation. We are a People of his setting up: It is not by Strength and human Wisdom, not by Arts and Parts, and Academical Acquirements; not by Power and might; but by the *Spirit of the Lord,* that we are enabled to overcome the Enemies of our Salvation, Sin, Hell, and the Grave, and to triumph in the Power of God, and sing the Song of *Moses,* and the Song of the Lamb, a Song of Deliverance. But before we come to sing this Song of *Moses,* there must be first a mourning State, an humbling of ourselves, and a bowing down before the Lord; We must say with the returning PRODIGAL, *Father, I have sinned against Heaven, and before thee, and I am no more worthy to be called thy Son:* And we may say, as the CENTURION, *Lord I am not worthy that thou should'st come under*

my

my Roof. The Power of Divine Truth muſt lay us low, and ſink us into a deep Humility; They that come not to hear the Voice of Judgment, can never enjoy Mercy of the Lord, nor know the working of God upon their Souls effectually to Salvation. Yet he will not break the bruiſed Reed, nor quench the ſmoaking Flax, till Judgment break forth into Victory. Where Judgment hath not Victory, nor Patience its perfect Work, People will not be patient, under God's Judgment. But *Zion muſt be redeemed with Judgment, and her Converts with Righteouſneſs.* This is promiſed to the Citizens of *Sion*, and *Jeruſalem* ſhall be the Praiſe of the whole Earth. Then they ſhall ſing the Song of *Moſes* and of the Lamb, a Song of Deliverance and Redemption. The Apoſtle *Paul* ſung this Song, after he was ſenſible of his miſerable State. *O wretched Man that I am! Who ſhall deliver me from the Body of this Death! I thank God, through Jeſus Chriſt our Lord. There is therefore now no Condemnation to them that are in Chriſt Jeſus, who walk not after the Fleſh, but after the Spirit: For the Law of the Spirit of Life in Chriſt Jeſus, hath made me free from the Law of Sin and Death.*

All are in a condemned State out of Chriſt; but when once in Chriſt, there are New Thoughts, New Deſires, and New Will and Affections; Then we ſhall ſhake off every Weight and Burden, and the Sin that doth ſo eaſily beſet us, and run with Patience the Race that is before us, and deny ourſelves, and take up the Croſs of Chriſt, and follow him, and learn of him a holy Reſignation to the Will of our Heavenly Father; and
ſay

say with him, *Not my Will but thy Will be done.* Thus God gathered a People in the Beginning, and thus he reacheth People now, and is gathering a People to this Day.

Blessed are they that live and walk according to the Ministration of the Grace of God in their Hearts, and that come, by Christ to be made free from the Law of Sin and Death. It is Christ alone that giveth Grace and Truth in the inward Parts, to make us free; and that giveth us Power against the Enemy; And though the Devil our Enemy be too mighty for us, he is not too mighty for Christ, who is mighty to save, and to save to the uttermost too, all that come unto God by him. Our Lord Jesus foiled the Enemy in all his Assaults, and conquered him by his Divine Power, even then when he *was led of the Spirit into the Wilderness to be tempted of the Devil*; The Tempter knew he was hungry, he knew he wanted Sustenance; *If thou be the Son of God,* said he, *Command that these Stones be made Bread:* But he answered and said, *It is written, Man liveth not by Bread only, but by every Word that proceedeth out of the Mouth of God.* Then he attacks him, and *taketh him up into the Holy City, and setteh him on a Pinacle of the Temple, and saith unto him, If thou be the Son of God, cast thyself down, for it is written he shall give his Angels Charge concerning thee, lest at any time thou shouldst dash thy foot against a Stone.* And *Jesus said unto him, It is written again, Thou shalt not tempt the Lord thy God.* Then again the Devil assaulted him, *and taketh him up into an exceeding high Mountain, and sheweth him all the Kingdoms of the World,*

World, and the Glory of them, and faith unto him, All these Things will I give thee, if thou wilt fall down and worship me. Then faith Jesus unto him, Get thee behind me, Satan; for it is written, Thou shalt worship the Lord thy God, and him only shalt thou serve. Thus our blessed Lord overcame the Devil, and vanquished him in all his Assaults and Temptations. *Then the Devil leaveth him, and behold Angels came and ministred unto him.*

This is an *Emblem* of what Christ will do for all his Followers, that open the *Door of their Hearts* to him: He will enable them to overcome the Devil when he does attack them; and to conquer that Enemy that hath sometimes overcome them. He will put upon them the whole Armour of *God,* and they shall be able to stand in the evil Day, having their *Loins girt about with Truth,* and having on the *Breast-plate of Righteousness,* and having the *Shield of Faith,* wherewith they shall be able to *Quench* all the fiery Darts of the wicked; and the *Helmet of Salvation,* and the *Sword of the Spirit,* which is the *Word of God. Pray always with all Prayer, and Supplication in the Spirit, watching thereunto, with all Perseverance.* Our Lord Jesus Christ will preserve his People under his Pavilion, and cover them under the Shadow of his Wings, all those that make their Applications to him, and obey him, and submit to him, when he reproves them for sin. If they turn from their evil Ways, they shall know his Power that overcometh the World, and all the Powers of Darkness, and obtain Salvation from Sin, and from the Wrath to come. Take away the Cause, and the Effect ceaseth: Can you hope to efcape the Wrath of God, while Sin, that is the Caufe, remains? This is as great a Contradiction as the Doctrine of Tranfubftantiation, that a thing is and is not at the fame time. O That People would come to be wife, and in this their day confider the things that belong to their Eternal Peace, before they are hid from their Eyes!

God hath given Chrift to be a Redeemer to us, to finifh Tranfgreffion, and make an end of Sin, and bring in Everlafting Righteoufnefs; and behold Chrift ftands at the Door and knocks if you open the Door of your Hearts and let him in, He will bind the ftrong Man, and fpoil him of his Goods, and caft him out, and take poffeffion for himfelf. My Friends! you that have heard the Call of God, and obeyed the voice of your Maker, and known the Operation of his Divine hand; you that have known the Work of Conviction and Converfion, and do Perfevere to the end, happy are ye. You do not know how foon God may Call you: The Time paft is gone, only the prefent time is yours. Now is the Accepted Time, Now is the Day of Salvation, let none harden their Hearts, now is the time wherein we are to act for Eternity. Now we have time and opportunity, for the faving of our Souls; we are fhortly to go out of this World, and the Lord will call us to an Account for our time, and all the Talents which he hath given to us. O that we may fo live as to give up our Account with Joy! It is the defire of my Soul that all the Opportunities and Seafons of Grace we now enjoy, may bring us nearer to God, and bring us to a better Frame of Spirit; that we

may

may acquaint ourselves with God, and be at Peace. Thus saith the Lord by the Prophet, *Your Iniquities have Separated between you and your God, and your Sins have hid his Face from you.* As Men come to turn from their Sins, and from the Evil of their Ways and Doings, they shall come to know the Mystery of God's Salvation Revealed to them. The Secret of the Lord is with them that Fear him, and he will shew them his Covenant. O Keep yourselves from Iniquity, and say when a Temptation presents itself, *How can I do this great Wickedness and Sin against God?* Do not Rush into Sin, as a Horse into the Battle, with a Brutish Violence; not Considering that Death is before him. Do not Indulge yourselves in any Sin; do not Gratify your Lusts, and Passions, and Appetites, but keep them under Government: Be of a Considerate heart and mind, having the Fear of God before your Eyes, that you may say with the Psalmist, *Psal.* 16. 8. *I have set the Lord always before me, He is at my Right hand, I shall not be moved.* The Enemy shall not move me, nor hurt me, nor prevail against me; He cannot ensnare me. If I set the Lord always before me, I shall not want Power and Ability to Resist the Devil and overcome him. Those that have set the Lord before them, he will be at their Right hand, and they shall know and Experience his Preserving Arm and Power in the time of Affliction and Distress, and Losses, and Crosses, and Disappointments: And in the time of great Calamities, God will be present with his People; even in the Night Season, He will sweetly Refresh them, with the Sense of his Love, and

Lift

Lift up the Light of his Countenance upon them.
Take therefore, Friends, *no thought for the Morrow, for the Morrow shall take thought for the things of itself, sufficient unto the Day is the evil thereof,* Mat. 6. 34. whether they be Moral Evils, or Providential Evils; the Evils we *do,* or the Evils we *suffer;* the Evils and Sins we *Commit,* or the Evils that God by his Providential Hand *Inflicts* upon us. Upon our Repentance God will gracioufly pardon the one, and Affift us by his Grace to bear the other. God will help us by his Grace and Spirit to overcome *Moral Evils,* to deny ungodlinefs and Worldly Lufts and Live Soberly, Righteoufly, and Godly in this prefent World, looking for the bleffed Hope and glorious Appearing of the Great God and our Saviour Jefus Chrift. What hope is that which the Apoftle there mentions? (Tit. 2. 15.) It is the Hope of the Glory of Heaven and Eternal Happinefs: That we fhall come to *Mount Sion the City of the Living God, the Heavenly* Jerufalem, *to an innumerable Company of Angels, to the General Affembly and Church of the Firft-Born, who are written in Heaven, and to God the Judge of all, and the Spirits of Juft Men made perfect, and to Jefus the Mediator of the New Covenant, and to the Blood of Sprinkling, which fpeaketh better things than the Blood of* Abel.

This World is but as an *Inn,* and we muft not think to dwell here, We are Travelling in the way to Heaven, the Undefiled way; and Glory, Immortality, and Eternal Bleffednefs are our Mark we Aim at; the Recompence of Reward, and the Eternal Inheritance. Chrift the Forerunner,

ner, that shall be the Desire of all Nations, is gone before us, and we cannot be Followers of him, if we walk in Pride, Envy, Covetousness; we must learn of him to be Humble, Meek, and Lowly, and bow to the Name and Authority of Jesus; to Submit to his Sceptre and Government. Let us Walk in the Way of Holiness, Humility, Self denial and take up the Cross, and be Crucified with Christ, and Glory in the Cross of Christ by which we are Crucified to the World, and the World to us; and then we walk in the way that Leads to Heaven and Glory; and look up to the things which are not seen, which are Eternal.

Dear Friends, take heed of Visible things; have a care that you Stumble not on things below that are Temporal; But look up to the things that are Invisible and Eternal, and lay up Treasure above against a Stormy Day. There are many that Build upon a Sandy Foundation, and not upon Christ, the *Rock* of *Ages*, the Chief Corner-Stone: Such are likened by our Saviour to a Foolish Man, which Built his House upon the Sand, and the Rain Descended and the Floods Came, and the Winds blew and beat upon that House, and it fell, and great was the fall of it. These were among the Foolish Virgins, they had Lamps and made a Profession, but a meer Profession will not do. The Graces of the Spirit of God, and the Life of the Son of God, leads to a Life of Righteousness and Holiness; that is the Oyl of the Lamp which they wanted. Blessed are they that have this Oyl in their Lamps; they that have it not, let them make haste to buy before it be too late, when time shall be no more. And you that
have

have it, fee that your Lights continue to shine before Men, and thereby Glorify your Heavenly Father. It is the desire of every honest hearted Christian, that this Light may shine and cover the Nations, according to the Prayer of the Royal Psalmist, that Antient Servant of God, *Lord Send forth thy Light and thy Truth.* Where must this Light go forth? It must shine forth of your Hearts, and Lives and Conversations, that People may say concerning you, God is with them, of a Truth. O Friends, answer the Love and kindness of God in this Day of your Visitation! If ever God appeared in any Age, he hath Eminently appeared in this of ours. He hath Called, and Qualified, and sent forth to Preach the Everlasting Gospel, a Company of Poor Unlearned and Illiterate Men, and he hath given them Power, and they have gone out in the Name of the Lord; without Academical Education, without Logic and Philosophy, Arts and acquired Parts, and they have declared the whole Counsel of God. I wish that every one may know the Day of their Visitation. They that will not bow to the Mercy of God, shall bow to his Judgments. Dost thou think, O Man, that thou shalt Escape the Judgment of God, if thou Despisest the Riches of his Goodness? No; God will Render to every Man according to his Deeds; To them who by patient Continuance in well doing, seek for Glory, and Honour, and Immortality, Eternal Life: But unto them that are Contentious, that obey not the Truth, but obey unrighteousness, Indignation, and Wrath Tribulation and Anguish, upon every Soul of Man that doth Evil; of the Jew first,

first, and also of the Gentile. But Glory, Honour, and Peace, to every Man that Worketh good; to the Jew first, and also to the Gentile; for there is no respect of Persons with God.

When the Pharisees sent out Men to ensnare and entrap our Lord Jesus Christ, they were Astonished at his Doctrine, and declared to those that sent them, *Never Man spake like this Man.* He had reached their Hearts and spoken to their Consciences. When our Saviour had declared Himself to be the Bread of Life to Believers, *John* 6. 51. Many of the Disciples departed from Him. *I am the Living Bread which came down from Heaven, If any Man eat of this Bread he shall Live for ever; And the Bread that I will give him, is my Flesh, which I give for the Life of the World: Then many of his Disciples, when they had heard this, said, This is a hard saying, who can bear it? As the Living Father hath sent me, and I Live by the Father, so he that eateth Me even He shall Live by Me; It is the Spirit that quickens, the Flesh profits nothing: The Words that I speak unto you, they are Spirit and they are Life. From that time many of his Disciples went back, and Walked no more with him, Then said Jesus unto the Twelve, will ye also go away? And* Simon Peter *Answered him, Lord, to whom shall we go, Thou hast the Words of Eternal Life?* We did not want *Words,* we wanted *Life:* Thou hast Living Words, the Words of Eternal Life dwell with thee. *In him was Life,* saith the Apostle *John, and the Life was the Light of Men.* And our Saviour says, *Mat.* 19. 29. *And every one that hath forsaken Houses, or Brethren, or Sisters, or Father, or Mother, or Wife,* or *Wife*, or *Children*, or *Lands*, *for my Name's sake*, *shall Receive an Hundred Fold*, *and shall inherit Everlasting Life:* Peter *said unto him, Behold, we have left all and followed thee, what shall we have therefore?* And *Jesus said unto them, Verily I say unto you, That ye which have followed me in the* Regeneration, *when the Son of Man shall sit in the Throne of his Glory, ye also shall sit upon twelve Thrones, judging the twelve Tribes of* Israel. I have sometimes told you, that Man's Travel in this World is like *Jacob's* Ladder; we ought to ascend every Day one Step towards Heaven: Every Day is a Step towards our latter End, and towards the Grave; let then every Day be a Step towards God and Heaven.

O you young Ones! It is my Hearts Desire and Prayer, That you may be saved in the great Day of the Lord Jesus; that you may now have an holy Tenderness and Brokenness of Heart, and that you may receive the Truth in the Love of it; and love the Truth as it is in Jesus, and serve the Lord in your Generation. It is not the Faith of your Parents will save you, nor will their well-doing recommend you to God: You must walk in the same Path of Life, and take up your Cross also, and follow *Christ*, and then *God* will take Delight in you, and consecrate you Vessels of Honour in his House; and you shall declare and tell of the Goodness and Loving Kindness of God, and of his wonderful Works, to the *Generations* that are to come after, when your Parents Heads are laid in the Grave.

O you Young Ones! I tell you once more, It is my hearty Desire and Prayer to God for you,

That ye may be Followers of them who through Faith and Patience do inherit the Promises; that you may receive the End of your Faith, the Salvation of your Souls.

I speak to you all, that make a Profession of the Truth as it is in Jesus. Let all that converse with you behold your holy Walking, be Witnesses of your Watchfulness and Tenderness, and observe with what a holy Fear, and Awe, and Reverence of God, you carry yourselves; that their Consciences may witness for you, and say, Well, these People are such as truly fear the Lord, and have Religion not only in their Mouths, but at their very Hearts: These are Christians indeed, *Israelites* indeed, in whom there is no Guile. This, Friends, is the Way to approve yourselves to God and Men, and to your own Consciences. God will then bless you in your Trades and Callings, and in your Basket and Store, when you do all you do in the Name of Christ, and to the Praise and Glory of the Eternal and ever-blessed God.

O my Friends, Have a care that none out-live that tender State that God brought them into in the beginning, but let every one of you stand fast in the Liberty wherewith Christ hath made you free; I speak both to you and your Children; Stand fast in this Liberty: *If ye be circumcised,* saith the Apostle, *Christ shall profit you nothing:* So I say to you, If ye go back again to the Spirit of the World, and be conformed to the World, Christ shall profit you nothing. Let none look back, as *Lot*'s Wife did, lest they also become a standing Monument of God's Judgments. O take

take heed of the accurſed Thing, the Luſts of your own Hearts, theſe Enemies of your own Peace, that would not that Chriſt ſhould reign over you ; *Bring them forth,* ſaith Chriſt, *and ſlay them before me.*

Bleſſed be the Lord, that hath given us the Liberty that we ſee this Day : God is pleaſed to renew his Mercies every Day, from one Seaſon and Opportunity to another.

It is the moſt ardent Deſire of my Soul, and I earneſtly beſeech the Lord, that you may all here preſent feel and enjoy the Bleſſing of our *Great High Prieſt* before you go. O you that know the Lord Chriſt Jeſus to be your High Prieſt, come and be Anointed of Him : The Ointment that was on *Aaron*'s Head ran down to the Skirts of his Garments. O bring your Lamps to Chriſt your Bleſſed High Prieſt, and he will give you Oil to fill them : Yea, he will ſprinkle you with his Blood, and bring you into the Holy of Holies. He is a good Shepherd, that will feed you, and bring you into green Paſtures ; and when you are filled and ſatisfied with the Fatneſs of his Houſe, he will make you drink of the Rivers of his Pleaſures, and bring you to the Fold of Eternal Reſt. But to the Wicked he will ſay, *Depart ye curſed ;* here is no Room for you in theſe Manſions of Glory. He will caſt them into Utter Darkneſs.

O my Friends, Let your Souls bleſs the Lord, and all that is within you Praiſe his holy Name : Let your Hearts and Tongues extol and magnify Him ; and let your Lips and Lives ſhew forth his Praiſe ; and ſay with the Pſalmiſt, *Holineſs becomes thy Houſe, O God, for ever.* I will Adore and

Wor-

Worship Thee in the Beauties of Holiness, with the lowest Humility, and highest Admiration: For Thou art worthy of all Honour, Glory, Praise, Dominion, and Thankfgiving, who art God over All, blessed for Ever and Ever. *Amen.*

TWO

TWO MADE ONE;

OR,

THE HAPPINESS OF MARRYING IN THE LORD.

A SERMON PREACHED AT THE QUAKER'S MEETING-HOUSE IN DEVONSHIRE-HOUSE, LONDON, OCTOBER, 3. 1694.

AT A WEDDING, BY WILLIAM PENN.

IT becomes the Sons and Daughters of Men to have a Sense of their Duty, that is incumbent on them, to the Great God of Heaven and Earth; and the Duty we owe to God, is to do all Things to the *Praise and Glory* of his holy Name. And happy were it for Mankind if they were duly sensible of their Duty and Obligation to their Sovereign Lord and Maker; and did set the Lord always before their Eyes, and acknowledge him in all their Ways, that he might direct their Paths. It greatly concerns us to have an Eye to the great Obligation we lie under to Him, who is our God, and Faithful Creator, that by his Almighty Power made us, and by his good Providence hath preserved us, in the Land of the Living, to this Day; to whom we are deeply indebted, both for our Being and Well-being.

They

They that have a Sense hereof upon their Souls and Spirits, they will take heed not to offend him, for the Fear of the Lord is planted in their Hearts. This is True Religion, the Fear of God, which teaches Man and Woman, first to eschew Evil, and then to do that which is good and acceptable in His sight.

The Fear of the Lord, it is said, is a Fountain of Life, which preserves from the Snares of Death. No Man that is replenished with the Fear of the Lord can be destitute of Divine Life and Comfort. Since the Secrets of the Lord are with them that fear him, he will shew them his Covenant. *Abraham* was said to be God's Friend, because he feared God, and God was his Friend.

O my Friends! It is not a Name to live; it is not the Character of a Profession; not adhering to a Party, or being of such a Society, or Church, or People; but it is the fearing of God, and keeping of his Commandments, and believing in the Lord Jesus Christ, and shewing forth his Virtues in our Conversation, that doth speak us to be real Christians. *He hath shewed thee, O Man, what is good.* O Man, that is, *Mankind*; the whole Race of Human Kind. God *hath shewed thee, O Man, what is Good; and what doth the Lord require of thee, but to do Justly, and to love Mercy, and to walk humbly with thy God?* Mic. 6. 8. Let us all take heed to walk in this Way, and that will give us Acceptance with God, and fit and prepare us for his holy Worship. *Abraham* was the Friend of God, because he believed and obeyed. It is not enough to make a Profession of Religion, and Godliness, and Christianity, if we be found

vain

vain in our Converfation, and to love the World more than God, and to be more careful what we fhall eat, and what we fhall drink, and what we fhall put on, and how we fhall divert and pleafe ourfelves than to pleafe God. Our Hearts and Affections fhould be fet on Things above, and not on Things below: We fhould with the Apoftle, not look to the Things that are feen and Temporal, but to the Things that are not feen, and Eternal. They that mind temporal Things will be difappointed upon a Death-bed; but thofe that fear God, fhall not only have prefent Peace, but future and everlafting Comfort. Let us all endeavour to be purifying our Minds, Wills and Affections, that we may enter into a holy Covenant with God, into a heavenly Marriage and League with him: They that are joined unto the Lord are one Spirit. As we come under the Teachings of God, we fhall be united in our Love and Affections to him, and delight ourfelves in the Lord, who only can give us, the Defires of our Hearts. The World paffeth away, and the Luftre and Glory of it, and all the vifible Relations and Capacities we ftand in: Let us then ufe the World as if we ufed it not; and let them that have Wives be as if they had none, (as faith the Apoftle) for the Fafhion of this World paffeth away. There is a time to Live, and a time to die; and as fure as we die, we muft be judged. Let every one of us endeavour fo to live, that we may give up our Account with Joy, and not with Grief: Let the Fear of the Lord poffefs your Hearts, which is the beginning of Wifdom. When Men and Women do that which is pleafing to God, and live in the Fear of God, and eschew Evil, and do good, they, in so doing, promote their chiefest Interest. The Lord takes Pleasure in them that fear him; his Salvation is nigh unto them that in Truth call upon his Name. We see God's Visible Care over all the Works of his Hands. Here in this World, his Goodness is extended to all, both good and bad; he is kind to the unthankful; he causeth the Sun to rise on the Evil, and on the Good, and sendeth Rain on ᵗʰᵉ Just and on the Unjust; but in the other ⸺ᵈ there is no shining of the Sun of Righteous⸺ ⸺ the Wicked and Ungodly; no Com⸺ ⸺ Holy Ghost, no Manifestations of Love ⸺ᵇⁱᵃˢᵉᵈ to them; but there is a Revelation ⸺Wrath, and the Fiery Indignation of the Al⸺ᵐⁱᵍʰty.

⸺ the very Prayers of the Wicked are an A⸺ ⸺ᵗⁱᵒⁿ, and because they love the World ⸺ᵈ, and esteem it more than Heaven, ⸺never enter into it.

⸺my Friends, *Seek ye the Kingdom of God,* ⸺ *thereof,* in the first Place, ⸺ *with all Men, and Holiness, with-* ⸺ *which no Man shall see the Lord.* Those Persons that so do, have a solid Foundation, they have a sure Bottom that they can stand upon; They can look Death and Eternity in the Face, upon this Bottom, when they *Believe in the Lord Jesus with all their Hearts,* and shew forth his Virtues in their Lives; having the Promises assured to them 1 *Cor.* 7. 1. That God *will dwell with them, and walk in them, and be their God, and they shall be his People. And I will be a Father unto you,*

and

and ye shall be my Sons and Daughters, saith the Lord Almighty. Having therefore these Promises, (saith the Apostle) *let us cleanse ourselves from all Filthiness of the Flesh and Spirit, perfecting Holiness in the Fear of God.* Now unto such, *To live is Christ, and to Die is Gain.* They live in Holiness and Purity, through the Sanctification of the Spirit, and belief of the Truth, as it is in Jesus, being Regenerated and Born again, and thereby made meet to enter into the Kingdom of God. It was Sin that first brought down Man from Glory to shame; Christ came down from Heaven and Glory, that he might bring Man out of Sin and Shame to Glory again ; which by Sin he had lost and forfeited. Our Saviour said unto *Nicodemus, Verily, verily, I say unto thee, Except a Man be born of Water, and of the Spirit, he cannot enter into the Kingdom of God. That which is born of the Flesh is Flesh, and that which is born of the Spirit is Spirit. Marvel not that I said unto thee, Ye must be born again; the wind bloweth where it listeth, and thou hearest the Sound thereof, but cannot tell whence it cometh, and whither it goes, so is every one that is born of the Spirit.* Nicodemus *answered and said unto him, How can these Things be ? Jesus answered and said unto him, Art thou a Master of* Israel, *and knowest not these Things ?* Art thou a Judge, and a Law-giver, and not skilled in the Doctrine of Regeneration ? Man being fallen from God, there is no coming to God again without Christ, and without coming from that which separated him from the Lord.

God made all good, and Man made all bad. Christ came into the World to make all good again

gain. Christ Died for all; but they only have the Benefit of his Death to Salvation, that die to their Sins. For Sin will still live against them, for all Christ's Death, that live in Sin, and not in Christ. Friends I desire that you may all come to a Sense of your spiritual Condition: The Lord is pleased to follow us with his Mercies, and with many Spiritual Favours, and Blessings: God is the Fountain of all Good, from whence comes every good and perfect Gift; with whom is no Variableness, nor Shadow of Turning; whom to know is Life Eternal: Let us live suitably, be sensible of his Mercies, and be fixed in our Obedience; for 'tis the Obedient that Eat the Good of the Land. Before the Deluge came upon the old World, God sent his Spirit, to strive with them, to bring them to Repentance. And this is our Testimony, 1 John 1. 2. 3. *That which was from the Beginning, Which we have heard, which we have seen with our Eyes, which we have looked upon, and our Hands have handled, of the Word of Life; That which we have seen and heard, declare we unto you, that ye also may have Fellowship with us; and truly our Fellowship is with the Father, and with his Son Jesus Christ.* This is a time wherein we are to work out our own Salvation with Fear and Trembling, and to give all Diligence to make our Calling and Election sure. We have now a Call to Repentance, and if we faithfully answer that Call, we need not fear a Call to Judgment; but we may, each of us say, with the Apostle, *I have fought a good Fight, I have finished my Course, I have kept the Faith; Henceforth there is laid up for me a Crown*

of

of Righteousness, which the Lord the Righteous Judge shall give me at that Day ; and not to me only, but unto all them also that love His Appearing.

Every one that cometh to God's Holy Spirit, to be led by it, He will lead them into all Truth: If the Spirit of Christ dwell not in you, ye are none of his. If we have the Spirit of Meekness, Patience, Humility, Charity, and Kindness, by these Virtues and Qualifications of Christ's working in us, we are brought into a near Relation to Christ, who is the only begotten of the Father, full of Grace and Truth. He is by Nature the Son of God, and by Participation of his Nature, and Adoption, we become God's Children too ; and by the Operation of the Holy Ghost, they that are born of the Spirit and partake of the Fruits of the Spirit, have clear Evidence of their being Children of God. Gal. 5. 22, 23. *Now the Fruit of the Spirit, is Love, Joy, Peace, Long-suffering, Gentleness, Goodness, Faith, Meekness, Temperance; against such there is no Law.* If these Things abound in you, you are free from the Condemnation of the Law. There are a People that bolster up themselves, and buoy up themselves, in not being under the Law, but under Grace ; but they are not yet come to the Poor Prodigal's State, *Father I have sinned against Heaven, and before thee, and am no more worthy to be called thy Son:* Nor yet to the State and Condition of the Penitent Publican, who prayed God to be Merciful to him a Sinner; nor to *Paul*'s State, when he cried out, *O Wretched Man that I am, who shall deliver me?* This shall be for a Lamentation, that too many are so

little

little Troubled, and Concerned, for the Lofs of God's Favour, and of their own immortal Souls; when the whole World is not fo much worth as one Soul. *What shall it profit a Man to gain the whole World, and lose his own Soul, or what shall a Man give in exchange for his Soul?* O how many do hazard their precious Souls for the Trifles of this Vain World? Let us all confider we muſt come to the Bar of Chriſt the great Judge of all the Earth; and if we be not found in him, not having our own Righteoufnefs, as the Apoſtle tells us; we ſhall be undone for ever, and we ſhall fee too late what we have loſt: And like Profane *Efau* (we ſhall be rejected) when he would have inherited the Blefling he found no Place of Repentance, though he fought it carefully with Tears. There is nothing will Remain then, but Chains of Darknefs, they that Loved Darknefs, here, ſhall be caſt into utter Darknefs hereafter, even the Blacknefs of Darknefs for ever.

Wherefore let all that believe in the Light of the Lord Jefus, Walk in it, and know and embrace the Day of their Vifitation. You that know your Maſter's Will, be fure to do it, and he will fay unto you, *Well done*: You ſhall hear that Joyful Sound, *Enter into the Joy of your Lord*. God hath Vouchfafed a Merciful Vifitation, a Day of Grace and Salvation, to the Sons and Daughters of Men: He hath brought us from a Gloomy Night, and the Dark Clouds of Ignorance and Superſtition, that our Fore-Fathers were Involved in, and the Day Spring from on High hath vifited us: We have had the inſhinings of Divine Light: Yea, God hath brought us out of Darknefs into his marvellous Light; let us walk as Children of Light,

in

in the Light of the Lamb of God. We live in the laſt Days, wherein that Promiſe ſhall be fulhlled, *That the Mountain of the Lord's Houſe ſhall be eſtabliſhed on the Top of the Mountains, and ſhall be exalted upon the Hills, and all Nations ſhall Flow unto it; and many People ſhall go and ſay, Come Ye and let us go up to the Mountain of the Lord, to the Houſe of the God of* Jacob, *and he will teach us of his Ways, and we will walk in his Paths.* Pray conſider what God ſpeaks to the *Jews*, that were his choſen People, and what he ſays concerning his own Inſtitutions, when they were Formal and Hypocritical in the Uſe of them: Iſa. 1. 12. 13. *To what Purpoſe is the Multitude of your Sacrifices to me, bring no more Vain Oblations; Incenſe is an Abomination to me,* &c. *Your New Moons, and your appointed Feaſts, my Soul hateth; They are a Trouble to me, I am weary to bear them: Waſh ye, make ye Clean, put away the evil of your doings from before mine Eyes; Ceaſe to do evil, Learn to do well,* &c. *Come now and let us Reaſon together,* ſaith the Lord; *Though your Sins be as* Scarlet, *they ſhall be as white as* Snow, *though they be Red like* Crimſon, *they ſhall be as* Wool; God is no Repſecter of Perſons. My Friends, Let us not be Outward but alſo Inward Chriſtians, in all our Solemn Meetings, and approve our Hearts to God, and worſhip him in Spirit and in Truth. Let us conſider that God is preſent in the Midſt of us.

All Nations do acknowledge that God is Omnipreſent; The Royal Pſalmiſt thus Addreſſes himſelf to God, *Pſal.* 139. 7, 8. *Whither ſhall I go from thy Spirit, or whither ſhall I flee from thy Preſence?*

Presence? *If I ascend up into Heaven, thou art there, if I make my Bed in Hell; behold thou art there; If I take the Wings of the Morning, and dwell in the uttermost Parts of the Sea, even there shall thy Hand lead me, and thy Right Hand shall hold me.* And the Prophet *Amos* tells us, *It is God that formeth the Mountains, and createth the Wind, and declareth unto Man what is his Thought; that maketh the Morning Darkness, and Treadeth upon the High Places of the Earth, the Lord of Hosts is his Name.* O how should we Live and walk as in the Presence of God! And set the Lord always before us, who is the Supreme Judge of the World; to whom we must be accountable for all our Thoughts, Words and Actions. But how do the most of Men live as without God in the World, live in a Contradiction to their own rational Natures? God hath made Men Reasonable, and his Judgment shall be most Righteous and Reasonable. The Lord hath given unto us his Light and Grace, if we do not improve it, and live answerably to it, we shall go down into Perdition, Therefore to Day, while it is called to Day, let us perform our Duty to God, and one another, that it may go well with us for ever.

These Things are of great Importance which belong to our Everlasting Peace: These are not *Chimeras* and *Enthusiastical* Fancies, but the great *Realities* of Religion. God hath been pleased in his Admirable Love and Condescending Goodness, to Twist his Glory and our Felicity together, and to require nothing of us, but what is for our own Interest and Good: He is Infinitely Blessed in himself, and perfectly happy without us,

but

but we cannot be happy a Moment without him; Yet we defpife the Riches of his Goodnefs, that is extended to us: And like a foolifh People and unwife, we are ready to fruftrate the Defign of his Mercy and Kindnefs, and to receive the Grace of God in Vain.

Let this Opportunity now before us, be carefully improved, in order to our Spiritual Benefit and Advantage. Let our Superlative Love be fet on the Lord Jefus Chrift, who fhould be our Hufband and Head. Let us Love him with fervent and Inflamed Affections, as becomes the Living Members of his Myftical Body; as thofe that are really United to him, and receive Vital Influences from him. We are now prefent at the Solemnity of a Marriage, which is a Thing of itfelf Joyous: But O let not our Joy be Carnal, but Spiritual: Let us rejoice in Chrift Jefus, who for our Sakes became a Man of Sorrows, that we might Partake of that Joy that is unfpeakable and Eternal. We may all live a happy and bleffed Life, if we will Live to his Glory that is the Giver of it, and fet our Affections on Things Above, and Live in a deep and daily Senfe of our Duty, to him that made us, and will make us happy for ever, if we be not wanting to ourfelves. When the Lord God firft created Man, he faid, *It is not good that Man fhould be alone, I will make him, a help meet for him:* And he caufed a deep Sleep to fall upon *Adam*, and took one of his Ribs, whereof he made the Woman; and brought her unto the Man, and *Adam* faid, *This is Bone of my Bone and Flefh of my Flefh*. Thus you fee in the firft Creation; God made Man and Woman in one,

he

he joined them both in one Person; then of One, he made them Two; and after made them one again: *Therefore shall a Man leave his Father and Mother, and cleave unto his Wife, and they shall be one Flesh.* Gen. 2. 24. It is of very great Importance to Men and Women, to dispose of themselves rightly in Marriage: For it is for Term of Life; and it is that which makes People either easy or uncomfortable in their Lives: therefore they must take Care to be equally Yoked, that they are one in Judgment, and in Affection. And when they change their Condition, to Marry in the Lord, that they may be meet Helps and Blessings one to another. God hath made us sensible of that Delight and Joy that is proper, both to the Outward and Inward Man, which makes us thirst after the Happiness of our Souls. This the Saints in all Ages have borne their Testimony to *David*, who was a Mighty *Hero*, and *King*; a Man after God's own Heart; he declares to us the Temper and Disposition of Carnal Men; They cry out, *Who will shew us any Good?* But this is the Language and Longing of the Saints, *Lord, lift thou up the Light of thy Countenance upon us*, *Psal.* 4. 6. That will make our Hearts more glad, than those that have their Corn and Wine encreased. The Refreshing Light of God's Countenance, and the Sense of his Love, is that which in all Ages, hath been the Consolation of the Righteous, ever since the Beginning of the World; and will be to the End of it. So (My Friends) we lay great Stress and Weight upon This, that Married Persons do not enter into that Relation with a Meer Natural Affection, or for Wordly Interest, or Advantage;

or

or to gratify a Carnal Fancy; but we muſt be in the Exerciſe of a Divine and Heavenly Affection; making the Law of God our Rule, and his Glory our Aim and End; Remembering that we are none of our own, but are bought with a Price, therefore we ought to glorify God, both in our Bodies and in our Spirits; which are His.

It becometh us to live as Strangers and Pilgrims on the Earth; For we are but Tenants *at Will* of the Great Lord; Let us paſs therefore the ſhort Time of our ſojourning here in Fear. The *Time paſt*, is Irrevocable; *the Time to come*, is uncertain; and only the *Time preſent*, we can call our own. Let us then improve it, while we have it; And in all our Solemn Meetings, let us have an *Awful Senſe of God* upon us, and *Love* him, and live unto him; for we are intirely at his Diſpoſal. You that are Strangers, and preſent in this Meeting, may obſerve the Order and Method among us, with Reſpect to *Nuptial Solemnities*. It concerns us to vindicate ourſelves from thoſe Aſperſions that have been unjuſtly caſt upon us. We have no Clandeſtine Proceedings in any of our Marriages, though we have been miſrepreſented to the World; We do obſerve that Order and Method which is ſet down in the holy Scriptures, which are our Warrant and Direction. We have divers Inſtances in Scripture concerning MARRIAGES, That of *Boaz* and *Ruth* is a very Eminent one; He ſolemnly took *Ruth* to be his Wife, as in the Preſence of the Lord, and before the Congregation, even all the People and the ELDERS, and *Boaz* ſaid unto them, YE ARE WITNESSES this Day. And

And all the People that were in the Gate, and the Elders, said, WE ARE WITNESSES, *The Lord make the Woman that is come into thine House like* Rachel *and like* Leah, *which two did build the House of* Israel, *and do thou worthily in* Ephrata, *and be famous in* Bethlehem, *So* Boaz *took* Ruth, *and she was his Wife.*

Thus let us proceed in all our Marriages, as in the Presence of the Lord; which none can do, but those that have an Awful Sense of the *Divine Presence*, which is graciously vouchsafed to his People in all their humble and solemn Approaches to him; Then He will Meet them, and Bless them.

I shall commit you to the Lord, and to the Grace of God that is given to you; For we are not a People so stingy, as not to own the Grace communicated to others, as if we engross'd and arrogated all to ourselves; We declare, with the Apostle, That *there is a Measure of the Spirit given to every Man to profit withal*. We are all intrusted with some Talents, let us remember we must give an Account of them. When we are convinced of Sin, let us depart from it, and live in the delightful Exercise of a Conscience void of Offence towards God and towards Men. Then we shall find there is hope for us in Death, and Fruition of happiness after Death. It will be said unto us, *Well done good and faithful Servants, Enter into the Joy of your Lord.*

My Friends, Consider now that Christ is Universally Offered to all the Sons and Daughters of Men, and his Love is, and is to be, extended to all the habitable Parts of the Earth; The Sun
of

of Righteousness will shine upon them, with Healing under his Wings; But this is the Condemnation, that Light is come into the World, and men love Darkness rather than Light, because their Deeds are Evil. He that hath given us the Knowledge of our Duty if we seek it, will also give us Strength to perform it, and work in us to will and to do, of his own good Pleasure. So that tho' of ourselves, as of ourselves, we can do nothing, we may say with the Apostle *Paul, We can do all Things through Christ that strengthens us.* Let us therefore labour abundantly in the Work of the Lord, and then our Labour will not be in vain in the Lord; *For if we be faithful to the Death, we shall receive the Crown of Life.*

CHRIST

CHRIST CRUCIFIED.

A SERMON PREACHED AT THE QUAKER'S MEETING-HOUSE IN GRACE-CHURCH-STREET, LONDON, OCTOBER 7. 1694.

BY GEORGE WHITHEAD, WITH HIS PRAYER.

AS it is the Great Concern, so it ought to be the Great Care of every one to have their Minds truly exercised towards God, in that Spirit wherewith he hath visited the Sons and Daughters of Men, for the gathering of People unto this the Testimony of Truth, in the plain Evidence and Demonstration of the Spirit, hath been brought forth in our Age and Generation: The Word hath been preached, the Living Word, whereby every one may come to a right Understanding by the Knowledge of it and the Sense of it in their own Hearts; the Entrance whereof giveth Light, and giveth Understanding to the Simple; and this is that which worketh the Heart into a believing Frame, truly to believe in him whom God hath sent. This is the Work of God, that ye believe in the Lord Jesus Christ, whom his heavenly Father hath sent, and that by believing he may be truly confessed as he hath been by a Remnant, whom the Lord hath raised up by his own invisible Power, and hath fitted and prepared them to bear Testimony of that which they have heard and seen with their Eyes, Which they have
looked

looked upon, and which their Hands have handled of the *Word* of *Life*, and the living Teſtimonies in our Days did ſpring from thence as in Ages paſt ; the Hearts of the Servants of the Lord were exerciſed towards him ; this is the End of our Preaching, to bring People to this, that they may know and be ſenſible of the Word of Life, of that which doth quicken and make Souls alive unto God, that they may come to know and experience that true and *Living Faith* that ſtands in the Power of God.

For which end the Apoſtles and the Primitive Believers were Witneſſes, whom God raiſed up as true and faithful Miniſters of Chriſt : They *Preached Chriſt* ; they *Preached His Sufferings*, they *Preached Chriſt Crucified*, as the Apoſtle declares, 1 *Cor.* ii. 1, 2, 3, 4, 5. *And I Brethren, when I came unto you, came not with Excellency of Speech, or of Wiſdom, declaring unto you the Teſtimony of God ; for I determined not to know any Thing among you, ſave Jeſus Chriſt and him Crucified ; and I was with you in Weakneſs, and in Fear, and in much Trembling ; And my Speech and my Preaching was not with enticing Words of Man's Wiſdom, but in Demonſtration of the Spirit, and of Power, that your Faith ſhould not ſtand in the Wiſdom of Men, but in the Power of God.*

The Apoſtle who was crucified with Chriſt, he that had a Real Knowledge of his Sufferings ; he that had a Spiritual and Living Knowledge ; a ſanctifying and ſaving Knowledge of Chriſt Jeſus, who was ſenſible of a Crucified State with Chriſt, and that in Weakneſs and Fear, and much Trembling, ſtill having an Eye to the Power of Chriſt, and

and to the Life of Christ, to bring them to know their Faith standing in that Power, O my Friends, this is the Design of True and Living Ministers and Preachers of the Everlasting Gospel; this is their Travel, and this is the Intent of the Labour of those whom God hath Called, who have kept their Station and their Habitation in that Life, in that Spirit, in that Divine Grace, which God through his Dear Son, hath made them Partakers of: It was Prophesied of Christ, *That when he should make his Soul an Offering for Sin, he should see his Seed, and that he shall prolong his Days, and the Pleasure of the Lord shall prosper in his Hand, and that he shall see the Travail of his Soul, and shall be satisfied.* My Friends, Christ himself Travailed in Soul, that a Seed might be brought forth to serve the Living God, and that he might see his Seed and the blessed Effect of his Travail; the Afflictions, Travails, and Sufferings of our Lord Jesus Christ were both Inward and Outward. Now they who know him truly, and have a living Faith in him, they know a being *Crucified with Christ*, a Dying with him, a being Baptized into the likeness of his Death, that they may arise and come forth in the likeness of his Resurrection. O my Friends, it is good for every one of you to be Serious and Considerate, and to be inward in your Minds towards God, that your Hearts may be affected with those Things which concern your Everlasting Peace and Happiness, that so you may come to be crucified to the World and the Corruptions of it, having the Flesh with the Affections, Passions, and Lusts of it Crucified, that you may live unto God, that you may so live in this present World, as to have

Boldness

Boldness at the Great Day of Judgment; for it is certain, the Confideration of the Judgment to come, is very terrible to many People, if they will but fuffer the ferious Thoughts of it to take Place in them; and the Reafon is, they have not made their Peace with God; they are not reconciled in their Minds, as they ought to be, to the Heavenly Gift of God, that he hath given to them whereby they may know the only True God and Jefus Chrift, whom he hath fent, which is Life Eternal. What is the Reafon *why* Felix *trembled* Acts 24. 25. when *Paul* reafoned of *Righteoufnefs, Temperance,* and *Judgment to come?* There was a Witnefs in him, that did anfwer to that ferious fort of Reafoning, and that was ready to fhew him, that he was wanting in thofe Matters of *Juftice, Temperance, Moderation,* and a real Belief of the *Judgment to come; And the Thought of it was Terrible;* There is a Witnefs near to People, if they come to examine their own Hearts, and look into their own State, and deal Impartially with themfelves; That will fhew unto them what they are, and where they are; That will fhew them what it is that hath made them unfit for Communion with God, and unmeet for the Kingdom of God; and that they muft of Neceffity be Born again, or they cannot enter into it: They are no fit Subjects for that Kingdom, if they be not fubject to the Witnefs of God in them, to the Light of Chrift within them, to the Law of the Lord in their Hearts, they are not fit for the Heavenly Kingdom.

And therefore, my Friends, let every one mind the Vifitation of the Lord; mind the Appearance of his Light and Grace in you; that you may therein wait upon the Lord, have your Minds drawn out of the Earth, out of the World, and out of the Lufts and Corruptions of it: That the Work of the Lord, the Work of a true and living Faith, Heart purifying Faith, all may be fenfible of: That none may reft themfelves contented, either only with a Notion of Faith, or with the bare Profeffion of Faith, either of God or Chrift, or the Holy Scripture; nor yet with being only convinced and perfuaded of the Way of the Lord teftified of amongft us, as many are: But let every one give up themfelves to obey the Truth, and look upon it as the Love of God, that he hath opened the Underftandings of Men by His Light and Grace: And that he hath affected their Hearts in fome Meafure towards himfelf, His Way and Truth: There are many have a better Opinion of the true People of God, than they have had heretofore: The Prejudice is allayed, and brought down in many; and the Enmity whereby they were made uncapable either of trying all Things, or of holding faft that which is good. So that as the Lord opens their Hearts, and inclines them towards himfelf; they depart from Iniquity: My Friends, pray mind the Appearance of his Grace, and the Working of his Spirit in you; that you may know the Fear of God to take Impreffion upon your Hearts, and to have Place there; and there you will feel it to be what the Scripture faith of it, *That it is a Fountain of Life to depart from the Snares of Death, and keep thofe from the Snares of Death that continue and abide in it;* and the Secrets of the Lord fhall be made known to them

that

that fear him, and he will shew them his Covenant; and wherein any are short in Understanding, and want Wisdom, the Lord will not be wanting to supply them, and help them if they wait upon him in his Fear; but if the Fear of God be rejected, and the Light that teacheth it, be turned away from, then People are not fit to receive Counsel and Wisdom, nor to know the Secrets of the Lord, nor the Things of God, which are only made known and revealed by the Spirit of God; For (saith the Apostle, 1 Cor. 2. 11.) *what Man knoweth the Things of a Man save the Spirit of a Man which is in him? Even so the Things of God knoweth no Man, but the Spirit of God.* There is no true Sanctified Knowledge any of us have of the Things of God, but what is given us by the Spirit of God; *For Eye hath not seen, nor Ear heard, neither hath it entered into the Heart of Man, the Things that God hath prepared for them that love Him; But these Things God hath revealed to us by the Spirit.*

The Mystery of the *Sufferings* and of the *Cross* of *Christ*, are revealed also by the Spirit: *What things were gain to me* (saith the Apostle) *those things I counted loss for Christ: Yea doubtless, and I count all things but loss for the Excellency of the Knowledge of Christ Jesus my Lord, for whom I have suffered the Loss of all Things, and do count them but Dung, that I may win Christ and be found in him; not having mine own Righteousness, which is of the Law, but that which is through the Faith of Christ, the Righteousness which is of God by Faith, that I may know him, and the Power of his Resurrection, and Fellowship of his Sufferings,*

being

being made conformable unto his Death. O my Friends, those that come truly to be sensible of this, they come to see and understand the Advantage and Benefit of the Sufferings of our Lord Jesus Christ, for the reconciling of Mankind through his Death, that we might all be saved by his Life: that we might all partake of Salvation, and of that Eternal Redemption which he hath obtained *for us*; that we might have it and enjoy it; that we might not rest only in a Profession that *Christ* suffered for us, tho' that be true; but that we may have a Living Faith of it, and a true Sense of it conveyed unto us by the Holy Spirit; that every one may truly esteem all that Christ hath done and suffered for the good of Mankind. I have known it (my Friends) with many others, for many Years; and we have had a deep Consideration of these Matters, and of the Scriptures of the Prophets and Evangelists, and of the holy Apostles, bearing Witness to Jesus Christ, both as to his Outward and Inward Appearance and Coming; we have been sensible of the Love of the Father, in giving his Son; and of the Love of the Dear Son of God, who gave himself a Ransom for us, to be testified in due Time, that he was the Son of his Father's Love, and that his Sufferings and his Blood was of great Esteem and Value in the Sight of God; and our Lord Jesus Christ hath given himself for us an Offering and a Sacrifice to God for a sweet smelling Savour: I have sometimes considered why this *Sweet smelling Savour* of the Sacrifice of the Son of God, did as it were, interpose between God the Righteous Judge, and the Offenders *Ill favour* of their many Iniquities,

Iniquities, and Enormities of the Sons and Daughters of Men, which they have committed: And that Judgment being come upon all Men unto Condemnation for their Tranfgreffions, fo that all who are in a State of Unbelief, are condemned already: Yet God the moſt Righteous Judge, with refpect to this fweet fmelling Sacrifice of his Dear Son, is pleafed to exercife Forbearance, and not fpeedily to execute the Judgment, the Wrath and the Condemnation which Mankind have brought upon themfelves, and have juftly incurred; but that there may be fuch a fpace and time for People to come to true Faith, and true Repentance, and true Humiliation, under the mighty Hand of God, under his chaftifing Hand, whofe Chaftifements are not for Deftruction but for Salvation, that they may be fitted and prepared for Mercy. Many that in a cuſtomary Way, cry, *Lord have Mercy upon us miferable Offenders*; and *Lord incline our Hearts to keep this Law*, and the like; They confider not what it is to be prepared for Mercy, but thofe Mercies that are extended to them, they abufe too many of them, God knows, and with forrow it may be faid, that many abufe God's Temporal Mercies and Bleſſings, and mifpend their precious time, and hazard their immortal Souls, and regard not God's chaftifing Hand when he puniſheth others for their crying Sins; nor do they confider their latter End, nor enquire into their prefent State; and they are not awakened by the Judgments and Terrors of the Lord when he doth by his Power and Judgments fmite through the Proud, that they might take warning, tho' many take little

Notice

Notice of it; nor yet are humbled under the secret Smitings, Rebukes, Reproofs, that they cannot but some time feel in their own Hearts, and which the Lord is pleased to send in order to soften them, and to make them tender and broken, and contrite and humble under his afflicting Hand, as they ought to be; and that thereby they might be reformed and effectually changed, that so they might experience the Work of a new Creation in Chrift Jesus upon their Souls, *That they might be* (as the Apostle speaks) *the Workmanship of God, Created in Chrift Jesus unto good Works, that they might walk in them.* Let every one consider and be sensible, that we are saved by Grace through Faith, but not of ourselves, it is the free Gift of God; not of Works, lest any Man should boast: This is that we own and prefer to all our Works, even the Love and Favour of God, and his Grace that hath appeared in Chrift Jesus unto all Men, that through the mighty working of his Spirit, we might be made sensible of the Love and Good-Will of God towards Men, that would have all Men to be saved, and come to the Knowledge of the Truth; he desires not that any should perish, but that they might Repent, Return and Live, and put away the Evil of their Doings from before his Eyes, and cease to do Evil, and learn to do well; then follows that sweet and melting Invitation, *Come now and let us reason together, faith the Lord; though your Sins be as Scarlet, they shall be as white as Snow; though they be red like Crimson they shall be as Wool.* Friends and Friendly People, I pray God that all may wait upon the Lord for this End, that you may all feel and know the carrying

ing on the Work of God where it is begun, and be true followers of the Lord through the Work of Regeneration; that where it is begun, none may faint in their Minds becaufe of Temptation, and becaufe of Oppofition; or becaufe of the Trials of divers Kinds that they may meet withal; but let all have an Eye to the Lord, and look unto Jefus the Author and Finiſher of our Faith; look unto him upon whom help is laid, upon whom the Burden of all our Iniquities was laid; he upon whom help is laid is Mighty, mighty to fave; *Him hath God highly exalted to be a* Prince *and* Saviour, *to give Repentance unto* Ifrael *and Remiſſion of Sins.* But how doth he give Repentance, fome may fay? We can fpeak by Experience fome of us, and declare that he hath given us Repentance by fhewing us, by his Light, the evil of our Ways; by difcovering to us the Nature of Sin, how exceeding finful it is; how offenfive to God; how injurious to our own Souls; and what a Grief to his own Spirit; and by bringing us to feel the Burden of it, and the Load and heavy preſſure of our Iniquities that we had committed, that we might be humbled under the Senfe of them; and this Senfe he gave unto us by his Love and Grace, and the poweṛful Operation of his good Spirit in our inward Parts, that we might come to know Godly Sorrow that worketh Repentance never to be repented of; that hereupon we might receive Remiffion of Sins, which our Lord Jefus Chriſt will give to all them that are truly penitent, and turn from the Evil of their Ways and Doings, and turn to the Lord with all their Hearts. So my Friends, Grace

waits

waits, Mercy waits, and the Loving Kindness of the Lord waits, and he will afford it, and vouchsafe it to us, if we will but mind to be fitted and prepared for it; if we will cease to do Evil, and learn to do well, and incline our Ear to the Lord, and hearken to his Voice, and obey his Truth. Therefore, my Friends, let none dally and grow careless and secure, nor have a slight Frame or Indifferency of Mind, but come and take up a full Resolution, through the Grace of God, to cleave unto him, seeing he hath made known his Way, his Light and Truth (thou canst say) to me in some Measure, therefore with his Help I will obey it, that I may grow in it, and partake of the Nature of it, and be a Witness for God in Life and Conversation, and not in Words only: A true Minister, a true and faithful Witness of the Lord Jesus Christ, and of his Power and Coming, must be a Witness, and an Example both in Doctrine and Conversation among Believers, and towards all People; and therefore the Apostle *Paul* speaks to *Timothy* as a Gospel Minister, 2 *Tim.* 4. 1, 2. *I charge thee therefore before God, and the Lord Jesus Christ, who shall judge the Quick and Dead at his Appearing, and his Kingdom, preach the Word, be instant in Season, out of Season, reprove, rebuke, exhort, with all Longsuffering and Doctrine. Let no Man despise thy Youth, but be thou an example of the Believers in Word, in Conversation, in Charity, in Spirit, in Faith, in Purity. Take heed unto thyself, and to thy Doctrine; continue in them, for in doing this thou shalt both save thyself, and them that hear thee.* O my Friends, we have known, since the Lord

Lord hath vifited us, thofe among us that he hath honoured to be ufeful and effectual Inftruments in His Hand, for the Convincing, Converting, and Edifying of others, that they muft Live as they Profefs. They that profefs the Truth, profefs the Name of the Lord, profefs Chriftianity in the Power of it; they muft have a Care to Live in it. I blefs God he hath made me, and many more, fenfible of fuch a Concern upon our Spirits, to live in that Uprightnefs, Integrity, Innocence, Meeknefs, and Humility, and Patience, with Long-fuffering, which the Lord requireth of us, that we may be preferved, that fo the Prefence of the Lord may be continued with us. I remember with what Holy Fervency the Royal Prophet prayeth upon this account, *Pfal.* 51. 6, 7, 10, 11, 12. *Behold thou defireft Truth in the inward Parts, and in the hidden Part thou fhalt make me to know Wifdom; purge me with Hyfop, and I fhall be clean; wafh me, and I fhall be whiter than Snow; create in me a clean Heart, O God, and renew a right Spirit within me. Caft me not away from thy Prefence, and take not thy holy Spirit from me; reftore unto me the Joy of thy Salvation, and uphold me with thy free Spirit; then will I teach Tranfgreffers thy Way, and Sinners fhall be converted unto thee.* Thefe are Qualifications and Endowments that do appertain to a true Witnefs for God in the World; he hath raifed up Powerful, Living and Effectual Inftruments in many Ages, that have had a Regard to Purity of Heart, and Conftancy, and Perfeverance in well-doing, and an Heavenly Converfation to adorn the Doctrine of God our

Saviour in all Things, and that are zealous to promote the Honour of his Excellent Name and Truth. I pray God, that all among us may be under such an inward and deep Concern for our Immortal Souls, as to see that all is well at Home, that we may experience a Sanctifying Work, a Purifying Work upon our Hearts, that we may be fit Vessels to enjoy and possess that Heavenly Treasure that the Lord hath given us, and not only to us, but to all them that Love and Fear him, and desire to be kept near unto him, and feel a Sense of his Living Presence, wherein is Life and Joy for ever and ever. So God Almighty that hath begun his Work, carry it on, and make it prosper on the Souls of his People, that they may be serious, and solemn, and diligent in serving him, and wait upon the Lord all the Days of their appointed Time, until their Change come.

My Friends, I could say many Things, but the Time would fail me to mention what the Lord hath opened to me; I hope the Lord will be pleased to give me further Opportunity. Let every Man that hath received a Gift to profit withal, speak as becomes the Oracles of God. This hath been the Desire of the faithful Ministers of Christ, to wait upon the Divine Oracle, the Word of God, that as Testimonies sprung up from them, they might be faithful in giving them forth, that they might truly and faithfully Testify to the Words of Life, whether it be in a greater or in a lesser Measure. We are not our own, we cannot contrive for ourselves, we are to be in Subjection to God, and live in a Holy Resignation to his Wisdom and Will, and have

our

our Minds ſtayed upon him, and wait for the Divine Counſel and Divine Openings to be given to us from Heaven: And many Times we have had in our waiting upon the Lord, Great Things diſcovered and given unto us, which are hard to be uttered and declared.

Every Faithful Miniſter of Chriſt that hath a Senſe and Feeling of the State and Condition of them in ſome Meaſure to whom he ſpeaks, he hath a Travail upon him, and is in a Crucified State, having been made Partaker of the Knowledge of Chriſt, of the Power of his Reſurrection, and of the Fellowſhip of his Sufferings, being made conformable to his Death, as the Apoſtle *Paul* ſpeaks, *Phil.* 3: 10. Such Miniſters are deeply ſenſible of that Vail of Darkneſs (and unpreparedneſs) in Hearers, that hath clouded the Minds of the People, yet they do not raſhly Judge and Cenſure them, but Travail for them; and ſpeak as they have felt and taſted of the Word of Life; I deſire all of you may examine yourſelves, and try your own Hearts and Spirits, that you may know how it is with you. When you examine yourſelves, take heed of Self-flattery. If Satan, the Great Deceiver of Souls, can by his Temptations prevail, he will not ſuffer you to bring your Deeds to the Light, which will make them manifeſt.

Friends, I exhort you all, as you Love your Souls, and deſire the Eternal Happineſs and Welfare of them, come to the Simplicity of the Truth, and love the Truth as it is in Jeſus, and be obedient to it, and be reſigned and Devoted to God, who is waiting to be gracious, not willing

ling that any fhould perifh, but that all fhould come to Repentance, and obtain Salvation through our Lord Jefus Chrift; defire to be a willing People as in the Day of God's Power, who is willing to do you Good, and is holding out his helping Hand to bring you nearer to himfelf. Bleffing, Honour, and Praife, be rendered to his great and excellent Name, who Liveth for Ever, and who alone is Worthy, who is God over all, even the Heavens and the whole Earth, to whom with the Dear Son of his Love and Bleffed Spirit (One God) be Glory for ever and ever, World without End. *Amen.*

HIS PRAYER AFTER SERMON.

BLESSED Lord God, and Father of Life, and of all our Mercies, Thou haft been a Habitation and Dwelling-Place to thy People in all Generations, who have trufted in thee, and waited on thee, in that Life and Light which brought the Dear Son of thy Love thou haft made known to them; Thou haft fent thy Holy Spirit into the Hearts of thy People; that they might fee their Way to thee, and draw near to thee, and daily wait upon thee in thy Fear, with all Humility and Lowlinefs of Mind, wherein they are capable of thy Teaching, and qualified to receive Counfel and Inftruction, and Wifdom from thee, the only Wife God.

Everlafting God and Father of our Lord Jefus Chrift, we have great Caufe to Blefs thee, when we remember thee in thy Ways and Dealings with us, and in thy tender Mercies to us, and to thy People in many Places, whom thou haft gathered by the Arm of thy Almighty Power, and whom thou haft called out of Darknefs into thy marvellous Light, that they might be a Peculiar People to thee, Zealous of good Works. Bleffed God, we have Caufe to blefs thy Name, and to fpeak well of thee, and to render to thy Majefty Living Praifes, and to ferve and worfhip thee with true Humility and Godly Fear, and felf Denial, and Sincerity, and Perfeverance. Vouchfafe unto us more and more of the Saving Knowledge of thyfelf, and thy Dear Son Jefus Chrift, whom thou haft fent, which is Life Eternal, that we may delight to draw near to thee, and enjoy the
Light

Light of thy Countenance, and suffer us not to live as without thee in the World; and as those that like not to retain God in their Knowledge, but let our Thoughts and Meditations of thee be sweet and savory to us, that we may be filled with Joy unspeakable, and full of Glory, whenever we come into thy Presence; that thou mayest have the Praise and Glory of thy own Works, and of thy Mercies and Compassions which thou extendest to us, when we diligently wait for thee, and Worship thee in the Beauties of Holiness.

O Blessed God! As thou art pleased to renew thy Favours and Mercies as the Morning is renewed, make us, and all thy People, sensible thereof, that they may dwell in that Life and Spirit, as will lead them to shew forth thy Praise in a well-ordered Conversation, let us give all Diligence to make our Calling and Election sure, and work out our own Salvation with Fear and Trembling, that it may go well with our Immortal Souls, let us know that our Sins are blotted out, that we may have Refreshment from the Presence of the Lord, being reconciled to thee through the Dear Son of thy Love, and Sanctified and Justified by his Spirit and Blood, we may be saved from Wrath through him; for if when we were Enemies, we were Reconciled to thee through the Death of thy Son, much more being Reconciled shall we be saved by his Life. Blessed and Righteous God, and Father of Mercies, it is only those that are truly Converted and Turned from Sin to thee, and that with full Purpose of Heart do cleave unto thee, that are sensible of Divine Refreshments, and that truly
know

know when Good comes, when thou art pleased to shower down thy Blessings as the former and the latter Rain. Lord God Everlasting, be thou near unto thy People, both here and elsewhere, that they may be preserved through all Temptations, and Trials, and Tribulations, that thou mayest suffer to come upon them, that they may be kept in the Exercise of a true Living Faith that worketh by Love that they may know and witness a Victory over the World, and over all the Temptations and Snares that are in it.

Glorious, Everlasting and Powerful Father of Life, in true Love to thy Mighty Power, and Excellent Name, let us be preserved, and in tender Love and tender-heartedness one towards another; that we may all enjoy that heavenly Salt within ourselves, that Divine Fire, that living and heavenly Virtue, whereby we may favour the Things of the Spirit, and discern things that differ, and distinguish the Precious from the Vile, that Temptations may not prevail, but that the great Enemy of our Souls may be seen and defeated, that we may not be ignorant of his Devices, but vanquish him in all his Assaults, and be more than Conquerors, through Christ that hath loved us. Blessed God and Father of Life, surround all thy People with thy Mighty Arm; let their Habitation be a Place of Safety, as in the Munition of Rocks, where their daily Bread may be given to them, and where their Waters may not fail, that they may rejoice and praise thy Holy Name in the Land of the Living, Prosper and Bless thy Servants whom thou hast called to labour in thy Vineyard,

yard, that they may be Inſtrumental for the Converting and Saving of many Souls; let thy Bleſſing ſucceed their Labours and Travails, that many may be turned from Darkneſs to Light, and from Satan's Power to the Power of Thee the Living God, that they may ſpeak a Word in Seaſon to thoſe that are weary, and faint in their Minds; and for the help, ſupporting and ſtrengthening of thoſe that are feeble and weak, and for ſatisfying the Deſire of thoſe whoſe Souls are breathing after Thee, that all may tend to thy Glory, and thy People's Comfort, and the Exaltation of thy Holy Name and Truth. Now unto Thee, O Father of Mercies, for all thy Favours, Bleſſings and Benefits, and for living Encouragements that from Time to Time Thou haſt afforded to us; we deſire to render and return to Thee Praiſe, Honour and Thankſgiving, with all the Living here and elſewhere, for Thou alone art Worthy, God over all, the Heavens and the whole Earth, Bleſſed for Ever and Ever, Amen.

CHRIST

CHRIST THE MIGHTY HELPER

OF

POOR HELPLESS MAN.

A SERMON PREACHED AT THE QUAKER'S MEETING-HOUSE IN GRACE-CHURCH-STREET, LONDON, MAY 12. 1694.

BY BENJAMIN COOLE.

WELL might the Man of God, the Man after God's own Heart, who fpake as a Prophet, and as a King, fay *What is Man?* When he was addreffing himfelf to the Great God, he doth with a holy Wonderment and Amazement at the Condefcending Love and Kindnefs of God to Man, cry out, *Lord, what is Man, that thou art mindful of him! And the Son of Man, that thou vifiteft him!* Really Friends, Man is a poor weak Creature, he is a very helplefs Creature; all the Creatures that God hath made, are in a better ftate and ftation than he, *unlefs he be helped with Help from above, from his Helper in Heaven.* He hath a great Work to do, a great Race to Run, he hath a great Fight to engage in, and he hath no ftrength of his own to do it, nor Power or Ability; but that is not all, there is worfe than all this;

this; HE IS ALTOGETHER HELPLESS, and tho' he is so; yet, HE DOTH NOT KNOW HIMSELF TO BE SO.

  O my Friends, This hath been the Travail of my Soul this Day among you, That we may all come to have a Sense of our helpless State, of our poor and low Estate. There is no Doubt but if we are poor enough, God will enrich us; there is no Question but if we have a *Right* Sense of our own *Weakness*, we shall be *supplied* with *Strength:* For there is Strength enough, and Power and Sufficiency enough in him, as hath been testified this Day. *Help is laid upon One that is Mighty to save* even to the uttermost: But who are saved by him? All they that come unto God by him, they know Strength, they know Help, and Power, and Assistance from him. But here is the Unhappiness of the World in this our Day, as it was in the Days of Old; *Christ was in the World, and the World was made by him, and the World knew him not: He came to his own,* (that was the Jews) *and his own received him not:* The Jews were his Peculiar People: It is true, all the World was his, both *Jew* and *Gentile,* that is by the Right of *Creation,* but the Jews were his in a more peculiar Manner: *You have I known,* saith He, *of all the Nations and Families of the Earth: I have not dealt with other Nations as I have dealt with you:* He gave his *Law* and *Statutes* to *Israel,* they were his Peculiar People, and Christ owned them as such. We have upon Record in the holy Scripture, a large History of the Noble Acts of the Lord, and of the wonderful Things that his mighty Arm wrought for that People;

People; he signalized his Love and Favour, and magnified his Name and Power amongst them; yet when our Lord Jesus came to them, (his own) *his own received him not*; and because they did not receive him, they fell short of the Glory of God; they did not believe in, nor follow the Captain of our Salvation, who was made perfect through Sufferings: They did not come under his Banner, that they might resist the Devil, and overcome the World, and be more than Conquerors; nor did they fight the good Fight of Faith, that they might lay hold on Eternal Life; they did not run the Heavenly Race, *(viz.)* so run as to obtain the Crown, they did not accomplish the Work they were called to, and the Reason was, *They did not come to Christ, nor would they receive him upon whom Help was laid.* And this is the Sin and Misery of the World in this our Age and Generation. *They will not come to Christ that they might have Life, and have it abundantly.* God hath a Regard to all the Works of his Hands, more especially to the Sons and Daughters of Men: He is not willing that any should perish, but that all should come to Repentance, and to the Knowledge of the Truth, that they may be saved: To such as receive Christ, (who is the the Gift of God) to them he giveth Power to become the Sons of God: If you receive Christ, you shall have Power communicated to your Souls.

But what Power is it that we want, may some say? What do we want Power for, and Strength for? What do we need Help for? O it is to resist the Devil, to make War against the

Enemy

Enemy of our Souls: We have a subtle and potent Enemy to war withal: *Your Adversary the Devil like a Roaring Lion goes about continually seeking whom he may Devour.* Are you not sensible of his Temptations every Day? Do you not observe how he prevails over the World that lies in Wickedness, and destroys the Sons and Daughters of Men? Such as drink Iniquity like Water, and Sin as it were with Cart-Ropes; such as let loose the Reins to their Lusts, and take their Swing in the Pleasures and Vanities of the World; not remembering they must give an Account at Christ's Tribunal for whatsoever they had done in the Body, whether it be Good or Evil: These are they that the Devil, the Enemy of our Souls, makes a Prey of: *He goes about continually, seeking whom he may destroy.* Blessed are they that are delivered from his Snares: He hath Gins and Traps to entangle Men and Women in; he matters not what it is, so it be made a Snare to them. He seeks to make their Table a Snare, their Trade a Snare, and their Company a Snare. Therefore it concerns you all to watch and pray, that you enter not into Temptation.

Man (as I said) is a Poor weak helpless Creature, yet he is apt to pride himself in his own Strength, and to Value himself upon his own Wisdom, and Parts, and Knowledge, and Experience, and to esteem himself highly for his Riches, Honour and Grandeur in the World, he values himself upon the Account of these Things which will not prove Advantageous to him in a Day of Trial. When the Enemy assaults, none of these Things can defend from his Temptations, none

of

of thefe Things can fecure us; no after all we are not able to fave and defend ourfelves from the Wiles, and Stratagems of that old Serpent: We have no Power or Sufficiency, we cannot fo much as think a good Thought, much lefs do a good Act of ourfelves.

Well, therefore did our Lord and Saviour fay, What I fay unto you, I fay unto all *Watch*, It greatly concerns you all to be a Watchful and a Praying People therefore Watch and Pray continually, for all the Time that we are off from our Duty, we are obnoxious to the Enemy: We ought always to be upon our Guard, and to ftand ready Armed, that we may Refift and Defeat him in all his Attacks. This is the great Duty of a Chriftian, Intirely to depend upon the Lord, who is always Gracioufly prefent with his People that truft in him, that are fenfible of their own Weaknefs and Poverty, and low Eftate, without him; he is prefent with fuch an Humble Soul; that is vile in his own Eyes, and hath nothing of his own to Rely upon; we muft not think to live Independantly as if we had a Sufficiency in ourfelves, but we muft always depend upon the Lord, that we may have frefh Supplies from Him. We muft in all our Conflicts with our fpiritual Enemies wait to have frefh Recruits from Chrift, who is the Captain of our Salvation, elfe we fhall fuftain Lofs and Damage. Now there is Help laid upon Him, that is the Mighty One, the Lord Jefus Chrift, who is appointed of the Father, for Salvation to the Ends of the Earth, there is a Gracious Invitation to all the Ends of the Earth, to look unto him that they may be faved.

ved. This is that which I would Press you all to, to come where there is All-sufficient Power and Ability to help us. I have told you already; It is not in our Selves, Therefore we must not depend upon ourselves, upon our own Wisdom, and Strength, our own Parts, and Acquirements, we must not go there, we must not have a Dependance upon any of these Things, but our Trust and Dependance must be upon the Lord Jesus Christ, *upon whom help is laid*; they that come to him shall not want Strength to save and defend them against all the Attacks and Assaults of the Enemy, and the Oppositions that they meet withal: He is able and willing to save to the uttermost, all that come unto God by him. Now we cannot come to God, but by Christ, and none can come to Christ, except the Father which hath sent him draw them, and we cannot come to God as our Father, and in the Name of Christ our Mediator, but by the Help and Assistance of the Holy Spirit who maketh Intercession for the Saints, according to the Will of God. Man by Sin hath darkened his own Mind, and clouded his Understanding, that he cannot see the Glory of God, nor come to the true Knowledge of God and Jesus Christ, which is Life Eternal, till God is pleased by his Spirit to enlighten him, and reveal himself in him, and to him: Now the Way whereby God discovers his Mind to Man, is twofold, *without, and within*. The Holy Scriptures without: and the Holy Spirit within.

First, We may learn from without what a Veil there hath been over the Understandings of the Children of Men, that they could not see the

Glory

Glory of God. *But his Arm is not shortened that it cannot Save, no, it is your Iniquities that hath separated between you and your God,* This we Learn from the Scriptures without us.

Second, But there is a further Discovery made to us from within, the Spirit of the Lord convinceth us of Sin, and shews us Effectually, that it is our Sins that have made a Breach between God and us, and have provoked him to hide his Face from us, and to shut up his Bowels against us; Therefore if we would draw nigh to God, and have him draw nigh to us, and lift up the Light of his Countenance upon us, we must not hug and embrace our Sins, but we must Love what God Loves, and hate what God hates, and submit to the Scepter and Government of Christ, who is of Right our Sovereign Lord, as well as our Saviour. *But those mine Enemies* (saith he) *that will not that I should Reign over them, bring them forth and slay them before me.* This is that Testimony which the Spirit of the Lord is ready to give you, when you are convinced of your Sins, and have a Sight and Sense of them; You must when you shall have a Call from God by his Spirit, do as *Paul* did, who was not Disobedient to the Heavenly Vision. You must not consult with Flesh and Blood, but with full Purpose of Heart cleave to the Lord, for if you continue in Sin after Conviction, you will grieve the Holy Spirit of God, whereby you might be sealed to the Day of Redemption, and then a Curtain of Darkness will be drawn between God and your Souls; this is according to the Testimony of the Holy Scriptures, *My Spirit shall not* always Strive *with Man.*
Though

Though the Loving Kindness of God is exceeding Great, yet it is many Times withdrawn, when it meets with ungrateful Entertainment from the Sons and Daughters of Men, when they grieve the Holy Spirit of God, and live in those Sins which by the Light in their own Consciences they are condemned for. When you are condemned in yourselves (under Self-Condemnation) how can you ever expect to be justified by Christ? I testify to you on God's Behalf, Those Persons that are condemned here, shall be condemned hereafter; and those that are now Justified, shall be hereafter Glorified; the same God that Justifieth, Condemneth also. *Those that* Do well, *shall be answered with* a well Done; *and those that do Evil, shall suffer Evil*, and be sentenced to the Vengeance of Eternal Fire, and the Wrath of God shall come upon them, to the uttermost. O blessed are they that believe in the Lord Jesus Christ, and live Righteously, Soberly, and Godly, in this present evil World, and escape the Pollutions of it, and are Holy in all Manner of Conversation; that so live, that the Light of Christ in their own Consciences doth not condemn them, they have no cause to despond at all; tho' the Lord may hide his Face from them for a Moment, they have enough to stay their Souls upon; the Lord will be nigh to them when Trouble is near, and lift up the Light of his Countenance upon them. If thou art not condemned by the Light of Christ within, tho' thou art in a low and desolate State, in a helpless Condition, Be not discouraged, there is Help laid upon one that is Mighty, that is able to save to the uttermost, all

that

that come unto God by him. O my Friends, If we have no ſtock of our own to Trade with, or depend upon, let us covet and ſeek after the unſearchable Riches of Chriſt, and let us rejoice in Chriſt Jeſus, and have no Confidence in the Fleſh, Art thou Poor and Deſtitute, and haſt nothing of thine own to Rely upon? O Keep in thy State of Poverty, there is Bleſſing pronounced to that State, *Bleſſed are the Poor in Spirit, for theirs is the Kingdom of Heaven*; He that is ſo Poor as to have nothing at all, he that is ſtript of all, and hath nothing to live upon, he hath enough to live upon, he hath enough if he be rich in Faith, for he is Heir of the Kingdom, and ſhall enjoy an Inheritance with the Saints in Light. There are many that are poor in this World, and have nothing at all, and know not what they ſhall ſubſiſt by to Morrow, This is an *Emblem* of that Condition, that the Lord is bringing his People into; they have no Stock of their own to Live upon. No, not ſo much as may ſerve for a preſent ſupply; This is the Leſſon that they are to Learn, to Live by Faith upon Divine Providence, for the Juſt ſhall Life by Faith: *The Lord God is a Sun and a Shield, he will give Grace and Glory, and no good thing will he with-hold from them that walk Uprightly.*

It concerns you highly to be a believing People, to live by Faith and not by Sight; and to walk worthy of the Lord in all well-pleaſing: You muſt lay aſide all Props, and wholly depend upon the Lord, for he will never fail you nor forſake you.

I have an Exerciſe upon my Spirit, and my Soul is in Travail for a People that are afflicted, shaken and tossed, as in a Tempest, this very Day: I would not have such despond, nor be disquieted, nor their Souls cast down within them; but hope in God, who will be a present help in Trouble. O let such lay hold on that precious Promise left upon Record, that they might have strong Consolation: *Isa.* 54. 11. *O thou afflicted, and tossed with a Tempest, and not comforted; Behold I will lay thy Stones with fair Colours, and lay thy Foundations with Sapphires:* You know there is no Foundation upon the Sea (where the Tossing is) for a Man to build on, and in a Tempest or Storm there is no Comfort; but God hath graciously promised to those that are so afflicted, tossed and shaken, as in a Tempest, that *he will comfort such, and lay their Foundation with Sapphires.* If you keep yourselves from Self-Condemnation, and sinning against the Light of Christ within you, you shall enjoy this Privilege and Blessing promised: He that feeds the young Ravens that cry to him, and cloaths the Lillies of the Field, that toil not, neither do they spin; yet *Solomon* in all his Glory was not arrayed like one of these. He will take care of such as cast their Care upon him: Therefore trust in him, and depend upon him, without whose Providence a Sparrow falls not to the Ground: He will provide for those that love and fear him, and hope in his Mercy, and he will give them all Things richly to enjoy. The fear of God is an excellent Grace, and a rich Treasure. *O Fear the Lord, ye his Saints,* (saith the Royal Psalmist) *for there is no want to them that fear him: The young Lions do lack and suffer hunger, but they that seek the Lord shall not*

want

want any good Thing: The Angel of the Lord encampeth round about those that fear him, and delivereth them. The Providence of God will surround them, and Salvation shall be for Walls and Bullwarks round about them, and his Almighty Arm will uphold and defend them. There is no time to be without Fear; I would have you put it home to yourselves: Consider how many Hours in the Day, and how many Minutes in every Hour, you have been without this holy Fear of God: They that are one Minute without this Fear, do break that holy Precept that commandeth us to *Fear always:* Such Persons lay themselves open to the Enemy: Blessed are they that fear always. *The Fear of the Lord is the Beginning of Wisdom:* This is that which will make us careful to please him, and fill us with a holy Dread, lest we should offend him: Those that Fear the Lord, he will encompass them with his Favour as with a Shield, he will speak Peace to them at their down-lying, and fill them with the Joy of his Salvation at their uprising. It is our great Duty to love the Lord with all our Hearts, with all our Souls, with all our Mind, and with all our Might, and to fear the Lord not with a servile Fear, but with a *Filial* (Child-like) *Fear,* that is a concomitant of Love, such a Love as is ambitious to serve him, and will constrain us to keep his Commandments. To such as are in a State of Poverty, Humility and holy Fear, the Lord will dispense his Blessings, and multiply his Mercies; and he will bless them, and their Posterity after them, and they shall shew forth his Praise from one Generation to another: These are the sincere Christians, *Israelites* indeed,

(like

(like *Nathaniel*) in whom there is no Guile: The Apostle *Paul* tells us, *such* are true Jews; *For he is not a Jew that is one outwardly, neither is that Circumcision which is outward in the Flesh; But he is a Jew which is one inwardly, and Circumcision is that which is of the Heart, in the Spirit, and not in the Letter, whose Praise is not of Men but of God:* These are such as *rejoice in* Christ Jesus, *and have no Confidence in the Flesh:* These are the *Sheep of Christ, that hear his Voice, and follow him:* The great Shepherd of the Sheep will feed them, and make abundant Provision for them, and lead them unto Living Fountains of Water, and they shall lie down in the Pastures of Life, and enjoy an everlasting Rest.

Therefore, *Fear not, little Flock,* (saith the good Shepherd) *It is your Father's good Pleasure to give you a Kingdom;* a Kingdom that cannot be shaken, an Everlasting Kingdom, and a Crown of Life, a Crown that is incorruptible, that fadeth not away. Now my Friends, All those that are Chosen and Sanctified by God the Father, Preserved in Christ Jesus, and Called of God, and led by the Spirit of God, as the Children of God; These are such as glorify God on Earth, and shall be for ever glorified in Heaven, where they shall join with the General Assembly and Church of the First-born, who are written in Heaven, and with the innumerable Company of Angels, and the Spirits of Just Men made perfect, where they shall sing Hallelujahs, and sound forth the Praises of the Eternal Blessed God, saying, *Blessing, Honour, Glory, Power be unto Him that sits upon the Throne, and to the Lamb, for ever and ever.* Amen.

CHRIST ALTOGETHER LOVELY.

A SERMON PREACHED AT THE QUAKER'S MEETING-HOUSE IN GRACE-CHURCH-STREET, LONDON, MARCH 11. 1693.

BY SAMUEL WALDENFIELD.

ALMIGHTY God, *Who hath made of One Blood all Nations, for to dwell on all the Face of the Earth, and hath determined the Times before appointed, and the Bounds of their Habitation: That they should seek the Lord, if happily they might feel after him, and find him, though he be not far from every one of us.* This is our Time and our Day to seek the Lord; and it will be a great Happiness unto all those that find him; *For whoso findeth him, findeth Life*; and that will be very excellent and comfortable, and a precious thing to every one that cometh thus to find the Lord, *they shall find Life to their Souls.* This great Visitation of the Lord to Mankind, is in Order to their finding of Life and Salvation, which is only through the Lord Jesus Christ, *who is given for Salvation to all the Ends of the Earth:* And it is required of all the Ends of the Earth, that they should look to the Lord God that they may be saved. It is our Interest as well as our Duty, to look unto the Lord God, and to

be

be mindful of the Day of his *Visitation* unto our Souls; For we are his Creatures, he created us, and it is but our reasonable Duty that we should serve him, and answer his Requirings in this World. This might be a great Motive and Inducement to us, that great Advantage that we are like to reap thereby, Eternal Life for our Souls.

And let us consider what a Loss it will be, to any of us, to slight the Day of the Lord's Visitation to us; We have many Instances in the Holy Scriptures of the sad Case of them that slighted the Day of the Lord, that neglected and rejected so great Salvation, that was offered to them thro' Christ; yet it happened so, that some did reject it, and slighted the Day of their Visitation; Christ saith He would have gathered them, and they would not; and not only once or twice, but *How often would I have gathered thee* (speaking to *Jerusalem,*) *How often would I have gathered thee, as a Hen gathereth her Chickens under her Wings, but you would not; therefore your House is left unto you desolate.* This was the miserable Consequence of rejecting the Love of Christ; and the same Fate will befal any of us, or any of the Children of Men, that thus slight the Day of their Visitation, and will not be gathered.

These are Words that are quickly run over in Peoples Minds, they may read them in the Holy Scriptures, but till Men and Women come seriously to consider of them, and weigh them in their Minds, That *their Salvation depends upon it,* their Eternal Peace and Welfare depends upon it; for if Men will reject the Way which the Lord takes

takes, which the Lord hath ordained, they cannot find out another to themselves; God hath sent his Son into the World, to be a Saviour, and if Men and Women will reject him, there is no other; *Besides me there is no Saviour*, faith the Lord; This may be applied to the Lord Jesus Christ, for he was and is the Saviour of Mankind; He saved the People of Old; it was said in all the Days of Old, He saved them, and he redeemed them.

Now Friends, That which is in my Mind, is, to speak a little concerning the Way of the Lord which he hath ordained and afforded to us, to obtain this Salvation, it is through Jesus Christ; but the great Matter is, That all are to make a right Application of it unto their Souls; For this Way is Christ, he is sent into the World and yet many may perish notwithstanding; if they reject him, if they slight him, if they will not be governed by him. Therefore it is necessary that every one of us do consider the Nature and the Manner of it, that so it may be effectual unto our Souls.

Now Man's natural State, separated (as one may say) from the Lord, it came upon them by an inward Depravity, an inward Decay and Pollution upon their Minds and Souls, going from the Commandment of God in their Hearts, and the Law of God, and the Spirit of God there; This is the Way whereby Men went into a degenerated State in the Beginning. Now the Way by which Man should be recovered and restored again, it must be by a Power, such a Power as can reach to Mens Hearts and Souls; such a Power is the Lord Jesus Christ, he is called *The Mighty*

Mighty Power of God, the Power of God to Salvation. *David*, that Kingly Prophet, *Psal.* 89. 19. speaks of him on this wise, *Then thou speakest in Vision to thy Holy One, and said'st, I have laid help upon one that is Mighty:* And *Heb.* 7. 25. saith the Apostle, *Wherefore, he is able also to save them to the uttermost, that come unto God by him;* Observe, it is *by Him:* So that here the Foundation of Man's Redemption is laid upon a right Bottom, an effectual Foundation, a sure Rock, a *Rock of Ages,* and the Foundation of all the Righteous Generations, the Lord Jesus Christ; but now it hath so happened in the World that Men and Women have been at a mighty Loss, in making a right Application of this unto their Souls; People have looked for Salvation outwardly many times more than Inwardly; Salvation is an inward Work upon their Souls, by the Spirit and Power of the Lord God.

You may remember when the old World was degenerated and gone from the Lord, in their Imaginations, and in the Wickedness of the Thoughts of their Hearts, which were only evil, and that continually; The Lord's Spirit did strive with them, to reform them and reduce them again, to bring them back again, from that State which they were plunged into, but it did not take effect upon many, because they slighted it; but they that were obedient to the Lord, to his Spirit, Counsel, and Wisdom, and Instruction, the Lord always preserved them, and kept them, and delivered them, as the Prophet said in the Days of Old, He was their Saviour, he was their Redeemer, *In all their Afflictions he was Afflicted, the Angel of his Presence saved them.*

So

So that, my Friends, it is a wonderful thing for Mankind, to confider the Way of the Lord, the Way that the Lord hath taken, Appointed, and Ordained, for the Redemption of the Children of Men, which if the Lord had not done, we had all been Miferable, we had all been undone, we had all been out of Hope of Recovery; for none of us could help ourfelves, there was none of us could deliver ourfelves, or redeem ourfelves; *But mine own Arm brought Salvation*, faith the Lord by the Prophet, fpeaking of Chrift. And faith the Prophet *Ifaiah*, fpeaking of Chrift in the 53d Chapter, *Who hath believed our Report? And to whom is the Arm of the Lord Revealed?* You fee Friends, that the Prophet did open the Matter upon a right Foundation, and in a right Manner, when he fpeaks of its being Revealed, it muft be an inward Opening and a making known of Chrift to the Children of Men, not taking Things by bare hear-fay: He doth not fay only, *Who hath believed our Report?* but he proceeds further, and fays, *To whom is the Arm of the Lord Revealed?* And then proceeds to give an Account how the Wicked did look upon Chrift, this Arm of the Lord, he that was to be their Saviour; *He was Rejected and defpifed*, faith the Prophet; *For he fhall grow up before him as a tender Plant, and as a Root out of a dry Ground; He hath no Form nor comelinefs, and when we fhall fee him, there is no Beauty that we fhould defire him; he is defpifed and rejected of Men, a Man of Sorrows, and acquainted with Grief; and we hid as it were our Faces from him; he was defpifed, and we efteemed him not;* Chrift Jefus was a Man of Sorrows, but when they say he was not Beautiful, and had no Form or Comeliness, they give a wrong Account of him.

Observe the Prophet personates the Wicked as well as the Righteous, thereby to make a discovery to the Children of Men, and that there might be a right understanding; The Prophet did not believe there was no Beauty in him, *But that he was altogether Lovely, and Beautiful, and to be desired.* He was the only Means whereby *Salvation* could be procured to Mankind, he was the most excellent One, *Mighty to save*; yet the wicked *Despised him, Rejected him, and hid their Faces from him,* and so they do now; if I should speak after the Manner of Men, the Lord Jesus Christ hath no Beauty in him, no form or Comeliness, why they should desire him; but this is the Pride and Arrogance of Man, the Wickedness of Man that doth so despise Christ, for you may remember the Apostle *John,* and those in his day, looked upon Christ in another Manner, they saw his Beauty, *The Word was made Flesh and dwelt among us, and we beheld his Glory, the Glory of the only begotten of the Father full of Grace and Truth.* There was Beauty and Excellency in him, and you may observe how the *Church* of old, sets *Christ* forth as *Altogether Lovely, and the chiefest of Ten Thousands.* Those that were the true Church, and the Spouse of Christ, they made Enquiry and diligent Search after him, such open the Door of their Hearts to him, and earnestly seek after him, as most Beautiful and Desirable; It is intimated there by the wise Man of Old, when he represents

the

the Church seeking after Christ, *I opened to my Beloved, but my beloved had withdrawn himself and was gone, my Soul failed when he spake; I sought him, but I could not find him; I called him, but he gave me no Answer: The Watch-men that went about the City found me, they smote me, they wounded me, the keepers of the Walls took away my Vail from me. I Charge you, O Daughters of Jerusalem, If ye find my Beloved, that ye tell him that I am sick of Love. What is thy Beloved more than another Beloved, that thou dost so Charge us? My Beloved is white and ruddy, the Chiefest among Ten Thousands, his Head is as the most fine Gold, His Eyes are as the Eyes of Doves by the Rivers of Waters, His Cheeks are as a Bed of Spices, as sweet Flowers, His Lips like Lillies dropping sweet smelling Myrrh,* &c. *His Mouth is most sweet, Yea, He is altogther Lovely: This is my Beloved, and this is my Friend, O Daughters of* Jerusalem. This she speaks of him. Thus now there might be some Hopes if there was such a Willingness to seek after Christ amongst us, and to be mindful of him, in this the Day of our Visitation, in which he is calling to us, in which Time and Season he is Wooing of us, and would gather us, that so we might be saved.

Now my Friends, the Way to obtain Christ to be the Beloved of our Souls, it must be from an inward Inclination in our Souls, we must mind it there, there he Stirs, there his Power reaches, there his Spirit comes, there he is Revealed, as the Prophet said of old; Let us ask this Question with the Prophet, *To whom is the Arm of the Lord Revealed?* This Jesus, have you known him?

him? Are you acquainted with him? Do you know his Revealing to your Souls? I cannot tell, saith one, how doth he appear? How is he Revealed? He comes by his Spirit, by his Light and Truth into thy Heart; And when he comes, the first Work he doth, He discovers thy Sin, and Reproves thee for it. You that know the *Lord Jesus Christ*, It may be said of you that he is *Revealed* in you, and he is visiting of you.

But this is such an unpleasant Way to the Wicked, that love their Sins, that delight in the Pleasures of the World, *when Christ comes thus*, then they will hide their Faces from him, they do not desire him, they reject him, they do that which hinders the Work of his Spirit in their Souls, and in the Hearts of many of the Children of Men. Thus they despise Christ, and reject him.

Therefore whenever he is revealed to you, do as the Spouse did of old, seek after him, open the Door of your Hearts to him, and let him in; For he stands there, as was hinted of old; *Open to me, my Sister, my Love, my Dove, my Undefiled; for my Head is filled with Dew, and my Locks with the Drops of the Night:* This implies that Christ waits upon the Children of Men, in the Night of their Darkness and Unregeneracy. How doth this concur with the Gospel and Evangelical Testimony? When the Apostle *John* wrote unto the Churches of *Asia*, he tells you, That Christ stands at the Door of the [Heart.] *Behold, I stand at the Door and knock; if any Man hear my Voice, and open the Door, I will come in to him and will sup with him, and he with me;*
and

and I will make my abode with him, and dwell with him. Thus you see how the Prophets and Apostles do *concur* in their Testimony.

The Lord Jesus Christ hath been pleased to open this Dispensation to us, and to make us partakers of it, I mean of the Spirituality of it: For here hath been a long time a Profession of Christ and Christianity in the World for above Sixteen hundred Years, yea, almost Seventeen hundred Years; but it hath fallen out so with some People, that they have looked more outwardly than inwardly; they have *looked at Christ Jesus as at a Distance when he is near to them:* So that it is an absolutely necessary Doctrine and Testimony to be preached to the World in our Day and Age, that People might be mindful of the Inward Voice of Christ to their Souls, that when he *speaks*, they might hear; and when he *knocks*, they might *open* to *him:* But this hath been wanting amongst us, this hath been a Loss and great Misery that hath come upon the Children of Men.

It is *the great Mercy and Love of God* in this latter Age of the World, that he hath *Opened* the Dispensation of the *Gospel,* in the *Nature* and the *Manner* of it, for the Good and Benefit of his People, if they would mind it and regard it; For Salvation and Eternal Life to their Souls, can come no other Way to their Souls, can come no other Way but in and by the Lord Jesus Christ, and you must all receive it in the Way that God hath ordained it; God hath sent his Son into the World to be a *Saviour:* And it was prophesied of him most significantly, That the Lord would give him for *a Light to the People*; I may say

most

most significantly, for the People have been in Darkness, and many are so still; and this was the right Way, but it was refused and rejected by many of the Children of Men; the People that are in Darkness reject this Way and despise this Way; so did they of Old, they Rebelled against the Light, they knew not the Way of it, nor lived in Obedience; yet the Prophets prophesied nevertheless, after this, That Christ should be given as a Light and Witness to the People, that he might be *for Salvation to the Ends of the Earth*; so that the Gospel Testimony and Message is, That *Jesus Christ*, the Eternal Son of God, is *the True Light which lighteth every Man that cometh into World:* Tho' he hath been despised and rejected, we must follow the Line of the Prophets and Apostles, and of Christ himself; and preach Salvation in no other Way, and in no other Name than in the Name of the Lord *Jesus Christ*. This is the Way the Prophets foretold, and the Apostles witnessed; yet we have much ado to reconcile People to this Doctrine of Christ, and the Day of God's Visitation.

Many Instances might be given from the holy Scripture, that this was the Way wherein God did visit the Children of Men, Luke 1. 67. Zacharias *was filled with the Holy Ghost, and prophesied saying, Blessed be the Lord God of Israel, for he hath visited and redeemed his People, and he hath raised up an Horn of Salvation for us in the House of his Servant David: And thou Child shall be called the Prophet of the Highest, for thou shalt go before the Face of the Lord, to prepare his Ways, to give Knowledge of Salvation unto his People, by the*

the Remiſſion of their Sins, through the tender Mercy of our God, whereby the Day-Spring from on high hath viſited us; To give Light to them that ſit in Darkneſs, and in the Shadow of Death, to guide our Feet in the Way of Peace. We read all theſe Things in the Scripture, That the Lord Jeſus Chriſt is ſent into the World to be a *Saviour* to the Children of Men; yet they did not mind him; *He came to his own, and his own received him not.* And when he was to leave the World, he propoſed it to his Diſciples for their Comfort; *Nevertheleſs I tell you the Truth; it is expedient for you that I go away; for if I go not away, the Comforter will not come unto you; but if I depart, I will ſend him to you; and I will pray the Father, and he ſhall give you another Comforter, that he may abide with you for ever, even the Spirit of Truth, whom the World cannot receive, becauſe it ſeeth him not, neither knoweth him; but ye know him, for he dwelleth in you, and ſhall be in you;* Chriſt is the Light of the World; but this is the Condemnation, that Light is come into the World, and Men love Darkneſs rather than Light becauſe their Deeds are evil; they do not *love the Light, becauſe their Deeds will be made manifeſt, that they are not wrought in God.*

The Light of the Spirit of Chriſt hath a wonderful Influence and Operation on the Hearts of Mankind, a wonderful Authority over them. It is a Diſcerner of the Thoughts and Intents of the Heart; for as the Light of the Sun outwardly makes a diſcovery of Viſible Things, ſo the inward Light of the Son of God makes a Diſcovery of the inviſible Things: The Light of Chriſt diſcovers

covers that which no Man's Eye can see. When the Light of Christ comes into my Soul, it is to convince me of my Sins. The Lord Jesus Christ is the Light of the World, and he enlightens every Man that cometh into the World; so that this concurs with the great Testimony of the Apostles themselves, saith *Paul* the Apostle of the *Gentiles, God hath made of one Blood all Nations for to dwell on the Face of the Earth, and he hath given them their Times, and their Seasons, that they might seek the Lord.* He speaks this to the Men of *Athens*; all people are visited, all Nations are of one Blood, whether they be *Indians* or *Æthiopians* or of what Country soever they be. The Lord Jesus Christ, the Sun of Righteousness doth shine upon them, and will illuminate them, as the Sun in the Firmament doth by his bright Beams enlighten the World.

So that, my Friends, this Divine Light and Truth is a most Noble and Excellent Thing. Our Lord Jesus Christ hath opened to our Souls his Everlasting Gospel, his Excellent and Glorious Gospel, his Gospel that brings the Glad-Tidings of Salvation, and reveals to us the Lord Jesus Christ to be the Saviour of the World. You know that *Life and Immortality is brought to Light by the Gospel.* The Apostles in their Day did Preach the Gospel of Christ under this Head, though it is much out of Fashion now a-days, the more is the Pity. The Apostles were moved with this Testimony when they went to preach the Gospel of Christ, saith the Apostle John, *This then is the Message which we have heard of him, and declare unto you, that God is Light; and in him*

is

is no Darkness at all. If we say we have Fellowship with Him, and walk in Darkness, we Lie, and do not the Truth: But if we walk in the Light, as he is in the Light we have Fellowship one with another, and the Blood of Jesus Christ his Son cleanseth us from all Sin. This Apostle writes to Young Men, Children, and Fathers, to all States and Conditions of Christians. The Apostle *Paul* was a most Eminent Minister, and had a Commission from Christ to go and preach the Gospel, both to the *Jews* and *Gentiles*. But particularly, he was made a Minister to preach the Gospel of Christ to the *Gentiles*; but how did he go forth? What Method did he take? What was his Subject? What was his Text? And what did he design to turn People to? When he was under Examination, he gives an Account of his Conversion, how the Lord Jesus appeared to him from Heaven; and he was obedient to this Heavenly Vision. I went forth (saith he) immediately to preach the Gospel. How did he do it? What Way did he take? I went forth (saith he) *to turn Men from Darkness to Light, and from the Power of Satan to the Power of God.* My Friends, this was the Gospel he preached, Rom. 1. 16. *So much as in me is* (saith the Apostle) *I am ready to preach the Gospel to you that are at* Rome *also. For I am not ashamed of the Gospel of Christ; for it is the Power of God unto Salvation to every one that believeth, to the* Jew, *and also to the* Greek. The Apostle you see, made it his Work to turn Men from Darkness to Light, and from the Power of Satan to God.

I wonder that the Gospel should not be more acceptable to all Christian People up and down the

the World; I wonder why it should not go through all this Nation! And why should we not all obey the Light of Christ?

Oh Friends and People! I do this Day *testify* in the Name of the *Great God of Heaven and Earth,* That the *Lord* will *Exalt* this *Light of the Gospel of Christ,* he will give it *Victory* and *Renown* over all. It shall go through all the Nations of the World. We have a Prophesy of *Isaiah* 60. *Arise, shine, for thy Light is come, and the Glory of the Lord is risen upon thee. For behold Darkness shall cover the Earth, and gross Darkness the People, but the Lord shall arise upon thee, and his Glory shall be seen upon thee; and the* Gentiles *shall come to thy Light, and Kings to the Brightness of thy Rising. Lift up thine Eyes,* (saith the Prophet) *look round about, and see all they gather themselves together, they come to thee: Thy Sons shall come from far, and thy Daughters shall be nursed at thy Side; then thou shalt see, and flow together, and thine Heart shall fear and be enlarged, because the abundance of the Sea shall be converted to thee, the Forces of the* Gentiles *shall come unto thee, the Multitude of Camels shall cover thee, the Dromedaries of* Midian *and* Epha, *all they from* Sheba *shall come; they shall bring Gold and Incense, and they shall shew forth the Praises of the Lord. All the Flocks of* Kedar *shall be gathered together unto thee, the Rams of* Nebanoth *shall minister unto thee, they shall come up with Acceptance to mine Alter, and I will glorify the House of my Glory.*

Friends, this is a most excellent Dispensation which the Lord hath given to us, therefore I entreat and desire every one, that they be mindful of
this

this Day of their Visitation, and that they would not look only outwardly, but inwardly. The Apostles went forth preaching the Lord Jesus Christ to the People. You that wait for Christ, he shall appear to you. There are many Christians that expect the Coming of Christ to be at the End of the World but they do not wait for the Coming of the Power of Christ into their Hearts now. But one Age may come, and another Age after that, before the Coming of Christ at the End of the World; there were many Ages to come when the Apostles preached of the Coming of the Lord being near, and at hand. The Apostle preached of the Power and Coming of the Lord Jesus Christ; of his second Coming without Sin to Salvation: The Knowledge and Expectation of the Coming of Christ is greatly wanting among Professing Christians; and I must tell you, the Want of it hath been the Occasion of all those Miseries and Calamities that are come upon the World. If People did obey the Voice of Christ, it would quickly reclaim them, and reform them; but People are not fitted for it: There are not many Preachers of the Coming of Christ, that preach it thus, even the Coming of Christ by his Light and Spirit into Mens Souls. This is looked upon by many as Antichristian Doctrine; they call it Enthusiasm, and *Quakers Doctrine*, and the Doctrine of the Spirit, they deride it, and mock at it.

God knows my Soul is sorrowful when I consider it, how People that are called Christians reject the Light, and do despite to the Holy Spirit of God, these Things have been the cause of our Misery and Calamity, and will be so more and
more,

more, till Men come into the Light and Spirit of the Lord God, and our Saviour Jesus Christ; till Christians live together in Love and mutual Kindness, as those that are led by the Spirit of God, as the Children of God.

Now I would offer this, and tenderly recommend it to you all, that you will henceforth mind the Spirit of the Lord God, and hearken to the Voice of Christ in your Souls. This is the Testimony of the Gospel Ministry which was once recommended to the seven Churches in *Asia*, *He that hath an Ear let him hear what the Spirit saith unto the Churches:* What difference is there between us and them? You are all to hear what the Spirit saith to the *Churches*, and to your own Souls. How strange and *uncouth* doth this look? How unusual a Form and Manner of Speech is this? If we should go through all the Churches in *England*, and other Countries, and when we come there, we should say, You that have *Ears to hear, hear* what the *Spirit* saith to you; they would be ready to Scoff and Deride, and say, here is a *Quaker*.

O that the Lord would give you to understand this, and open all your Hearts, that you may hear the Voice of Christ, and what the Spirit saith to you, and to the Churches, least Misery and Calamity overtake you, and that will be very sad indeed, if the Day of your Visitation go over your Heads, and you will not be gathered: I beseech every one of you to mind the Day of your Visitation; turn to the Lord your God with all your Hearts, and have regard to the Voice of Christ, and his Spirit within you. It was said of of old, that *they which are led by the Spirit of God; are the Sons of God; and they that have not the Spirit of Christ, are none of his.* This I am sure is Apostolical Doctrine, yet how little is this regarded and preached now a-days? How little do People mind the Spirit of God? How little are they led by the Spirit, or walk by it, as the Children of God. *They that have not the Spirit of Christ, are none of his,* they that are not *Redeemed by Christ,* by the Precious *Blood* of Christ, that have not his Spirit. The Spirit of Christ is able to wash away thine, and mine, and every Bodys *Sins.* The Spirit of Christ came at the beginning into our Souls, and we were Baptized by it, and Regenerated by it.

Oh my Friends! if those that are called Christians up and down the World were faithful to the Spirit of Christ, the Gospel would flourish, the *Jews* would be brought Home; for unto this must all the *Nations* of the World be Gathered. They that come to be saved, must walk in the *Spirit.* They that will be *Eternally saved from Sin and Hell,* must walk in the Light of the Lord, and in the Light of the Lamb.

And so my Friends, to this Light I shall leave you; the Lord give you Understanding, that you may prize the Day of your Visitation, and know a being Gathered into the Light of the Lord, and be Baptized by the Spirit of God, and Gathered into his Kingdom; this will be an excellent Portion to you: But if you be not Gathered, then Calamity and Distress will come upon you, as it did upon *Jerusalem* of Old, and the Things that belong to your Peace shall be hid from your Eyes.

Oh

Oh that the *Lord of infinite Mercy* would incline *every Heart* to seek him, that they might find him, *for he is not far from every one of us; for in him we live, and move, and have our Being, for we are his Off-spring,* as certain of the Old Poets and Philosophers did believe, and was signified unto us; so the Wise Men of Old that did not make a Profession of Christ, they did see it their Duty, and had some understanding of the Way that God would take with the Children of Men. The *Jews* were in Expectation of this; it was their own Prophets that prophesied of the *Messiah* on this wise, *That when he was come, they would despise him, and reject him, and would not have him to* Rule *over them,* that is, in their Hearts. Christ did not come into the World to *Rule* over Peoples Bodies only, but over their Minds and Hearts; *My Son give me thine Heart.* He hath taught us to pray for this; *Thy Kingdom come; thy Will be done: The Kingdom of God is within you.*

Many Parables Christ spake and used in his preaching, but Time would fail me to mention them: Christ spoke these in his Gospel, that you might all mind the Day of your Visitation, and be Gathered into the Spirit of the Lord; Gathered to the Lord God of Heaven and Earth, and in and through the Lord Jesus Christ have Eternal Life and Salvation, that God may be your Portion, your Lot, and Inheritance, when you shall go out of this World, and be no more seen of the Children of Men.

F I N I S.

www.ingramcontent.com/pod-product-compliance
Lightning Source LLC
Chambersburg PA
CBHW031831230426
43669CB00009B/1304